THE MUSIC IS YOU

A
Guide
to
Thinking Less
and
Feeling More

Rosita Perez

Artwork: Jayne M. Massaro
Cover Photo: Robert W. Becker

Trudy Knox, Publisher
Granville, Ohio

For Ray, who heard the music in me before I did

For Mama, who left me the lyrics

For Rita, Rachel and Robin, who made the singing fun

CONTENTS

FOREWORD 1

INTRODUCTION 2

REFLECTIONS 3
    Estate Planning 4
    The Dreamers 5
    Wing-Walking 6
    Beyond the Rainbow 7
    A Day Away 8
    The Electric Company 9
    Compromises 10
    Enlightenment 11
    Burn-Out 12
    Religion 13
    If I Had My Life to Live Over 14

FEELINGS 15
    Peaceful Insecurity 16
    Image 17
    The Other Side of the Coin 18
    Programming 19
    Passion 20

CHILDREN 21
    The Competition 22
    What You See Is What You Don't Get 23
    Homework 24
    The Little Acorn 25
    The Twig and the Tree 26
    The Law of Gravity 27
    Priorities 28

PETS 29
    Of Lice and Men 30
    Conditioning 31

MARRIAGE 32
    Very Old Spice 33
    Reality vs. The Media 34
    Creative Problem Solving 35
    I'm For Men's Lib 36
    Anger 37

WORK 38
    The Search 39
    Distractions 40
    Payment Due 41
    The Do-Gooders 42
    Let's Pretend 43
    Legacy 44
    Goal Setting 45
    Perfectionism 46
    The Internal Barometer 47
    Who's Who? 48

STRENGTHS AND INADEQUACIES 49
    Success 50
    I Don't Know What I Want to Be When I Grow Up 51
    Orgies 52
    Character 53
    Fear 54
    The Desert Island 55
    Pawns 56
    Assumptions 57

CONTENTS (continued)

A Star Is <u>Not</u> Born... 58
Mrs. Clean 59
SORROW 60
    The Psychologist.. 61
    Hobbies 62
    The Existential Moment 63
    Funerals 65
    Dreams and Nightmares 66
    The Eyes Have It 67
    Coincidences... 68
PARENTHOOD.. 69
    I Said It Couldn't Be Done............................. 70
    Imprinting 71
    Witness for the Persecution 72
    The Child Abusers 73
    Love 74
SEXUALITY.. 75
    The Guru.. 76
    Meta-Communications................................... 78
    Being There 79
    Maturity 80
FAMILY 81
    Flower Power 82
    Little Brother.. 83
    The New-Born 84
    My Son, The Doctor 85
FRIENDS 86
    The Rich Man... 87
    The Girlfriend... 88
    Friendship 89
TEACHERS.. 90
    Education 91
    "Hey Man, Like Wow!"................................. 92
    The System 93
STRANGERS 94
    Wisdom 95
    Anonymous Angels..................................... 96
    Intelligence.. 97
    Prejudice 98
    Gay and Gray 99
THE PAST 100
    The Silent Scream 101
    Grass...102
    Ghosts and Goblins 103
    Yesterday's Tape and Today's Hype 104
    Gifts...105
    The Home Town Neighbor.............................106
    "A Little Child Shall Lead Them" 107
    Roots...108
    Dichotomies 109
THE UNEXPECTED...111
    On Doing and Being 112
    The Yin and Yang of It................................113
    Close Encounters......................................115
    Afterthought 118
    The Music Lesson 119

FOREWORD

As a man whose background fairly shouts Machismo —
boxer, Marine, author of *Tough-minded Management*,
but who finally perceived the strength, power, practical-
ity and grace of vulnerably expressing human emotions,
I recommend this beautiful book to every man, woman
and child who has ever asked: "What's it all about?"

What a mistake it would be for the "Macho Man" to
avoid this book because it is written by a sentimental,
sensitive and compassionate woman. For it is a book
for all ages, all genders, all backgrounds.

EXPECT THE BEST! You'll find it here.

                Joe Batten
                Chairman of the Board
                BATTEN, BATTEN, HUDSON & SWAB, INC.

INTRODUCTION

THE MUSIC IS YOU is a compilation of my feelings, experiences and thoughts. Its value for you will only exist if you recognize a bit of yourself between the pages and end up smiling a little more, crying a little less, and feeling a little less alone.

Being human is scary sometimes. The irony is that it is only when we embrace our .greatest fears, that we end up with a guide that opens up the wonder of the universe and the harmony in the world around us. Gradually, we are part of a brave new world. Not because the world has changed, but because we have and I find that to be an exciting, exhilarating, life-transforming, hopeful thought.

Rosita Perez
Brandon, Florida
1983

Preface to the Second Edition

Two years and many lovely letters later, there are two lines that appear over and over again:

"I laughed and I cried reading your book."

"I feel you've been peeking over my shoulder as I've gone through life."

How comforting to know we are not alone. Let us continue to sing the songs of life that sound melodious to us. And to share them with all who want to harmonize.

Rosita

Creative Living Programs, Inc.   813-685-8267
756 Fortuna Drive
Brandon, Florida 33511
1985

ESTATE PLANNING

Homes, cars, money, stocks, bonds, jewelry.

Those are the precious items we enumerate in our wills. I'm looking for an attorney who will help me add a codicil to mine in order to bequeath my hugs, my music, my smiles, and a bit of my hope. I plan to take my tears and fears and insecurities with me. The world has enough of those.

WHAT ARE YOU LEAVING BEHIND?

THE DREAMERS

We dilute our dreams when they are shared prematurely with others. They don't see what we are envisioning. And so, when they smile and say, "That's nice," we die a little inside, because their eyes are saying, "Ridiculous!"

Why do we set ourselves up for such psychic sabotage? Are you still waiting for approval before you sing your songs? Will you risk making your own kind of music — alone if necessary — or must you have the safety of the chorus with all the notes written for you?

"NO GUTS, NO GLORY" APPLIES TO A LOT MORE THAN SPORTS.

WING-WALKING

"Never leave hold of what you've got until you've got hold of something else." I read that first law of wing-walking long ago. That is a safe and boring way to go through life. Unless I let go completely, my energies are so depleted from the effort of holding on that I never really give my all to my next goal. It is only in letting go that I progress.

How about you?

What is it that you no longer want that you're still hanging on to? And how much longer will you continue to hold yourself back in the process?

Go for it.

With fun.
 With enthusiasm.
  With gusto.   (This is beginning to sound like a
   beer commercial)
    With faith.
     With a thankful heart.

Nothing and no one will stop you. What you want is out there waiting for you to claim it.

ONCE YOU STOP SABOTAGING YOURSELF AND GET OUT OF YOUR OWN WAY, THE PATH IS CLEAR.

BEYOND THE RAINBOW

Have you noticed how often our society is reflected in a song? Forty years ago we were singing a song that admonished us to follow the yellow brick road — and if you listened intently, you could almost hear the cadence count of all the feet marching in unison.

That doesn't apply today. That is why now the lyrics were rewritten to give us the message to "ease on down the road". I don't know about you, but that feels a lot more comfortable to me.

Ask most people what is at the end of the yellow brick road and they will answer, "The Land of OZ" or "The Wizard". The only thing I ever found at the end of the yellow brick road was more yellow bricks.

Have you got your Master's?
Are you working on your Ph.D.?
You've got the Doctorate?
Have you published?
It's publish or perish.

I GUESS THAT IS WHY IT BECAME IMPERATIVE THAT I GET OFF THAT BUSY HIGHWAY AND JUST FOLLOW WHEREVER THE MUSIC LEADS. THIS PATH IS SO SCENIC AND BEAUTIFUL. THERE IS NO ROAD MAP AND THAT IS WHAT MAKES THE TRIP SUCH AN ADVENTURE.

A DAY AWAY

"Today is the first day of the rest of your life." You've read that, I'm sure.

I heard a psychologist say that he doesn't live his life that way. If today were the first day of the rest of his life, it would give him all kinds of time to do what he really wants to do, and he would probably procrastinate — since he'd have his whole life ahead of him. He said he lives as if today were the last day of his life.

As I watched him on the interview show, I decided that although I agreed with his first statement, the second one didn't apply to me. If today were the last day of my life, I would not be sitting at this typewriter wondering why I never took a course in writing. And I doubt the psychologist would be on TV plugging his latest book if this were his last day, and he knew it.

I would be hugging my husband and kids, telling them how special it has been to spend all these years with them. I'd be on the phone running up a horrendous phone bill calling up people all over the world to let them know how much I've loved them and what a difference they have made in my life.

I've decided to live my life as if today were the next to the last day of the rest of my life. That means that today I will do what I feel needs doing because I've always got tomorrow.

Just about now, a little voice whispers, "But tomorrow may never come." So be it. I need to live as if it will.

BESIDES, IF I LIVE 10,000 MORE DAYS, I'LL BE RIGHT 9,999 TIMES AND WRONG ONLY ONCE.

THE ELECTRIC COMPANY

You remember the song that talks about waiting by your window for someone to sing you his song?

That's a terrible way to go through life. What if I sit by my window and no one comes? Or suppose they pass by and decide not to sing their songs for me? I'm much too impatient to do that. I will risk approaching someone and ask if they'd like to listen to my song. And if they say, "No," I'll accept it as an opinion instead of a rejection and go find someone else who will. When it is really right, I will hear their lyrics, too, and then we will be mutually enriched because we will have shared each other's inner music.

I'm aware Debby Boone was referring to a Higher Power in her life when she made that hit record. That is the only way that lyric about "You Light Up My Life" makes sense to me. Our light must come from within so that wherever we go, it is. That ensures that no one else's absence will cause our power failure. I learned that painful lesson during the cold, bleak winters of my soul when the music froze inside me.

I prefer the philosophy expressed in Kenny Rogers' recording, "You Decorated My Life". Now that, I can live with.

SUDDEN THOUGHT: If I believe what I've just written, why do I shiver at the thought that my husband might die before I do? Certainly he has been more than decoration in my life. Will I be so glib with my opinions then? Probably not.

BUT I PRAY I WILL STILL HAVE A SONG TO SING AND ENOUGH LIGHT TO SEE ME THROUGH.

COMPROMISES

Somewhere on this planet are people who walk by a bakery shop window and don't salivate. They look at pepperoni pizzas with disdain. They don't know what a Reese's peanut butter cup is. They don't get excited when the Girl Scout appears at their door with Samoan cookies.

And then there are those like me.

"I'll become a vegetarian," I thought.

Six pears, half a loaf of bread with butter and one-fourth of a watermelon later, I realized that the answer to weight control was not that simple.

Maybe the most many of us will do is make a compromise with life. No more size 18 with swollen feet and gangrene of the lower extremeties from wearing panty hose. But no more size 8 either — drinking diet soda that tastes like bug juice. Gradually, I have accepted that there are worse fates than a size 12.

WHERE DID WE GET THE IDEA THAT PERFECTION WAS A PHYSICAL THING?

ENLIGHTENMENT

The plane was cruising at 35,000 feet and it was 7 p.m. over Ohio. The panorama on the left side was breathtaking. As the sun set, it painted orange and red streaks across the middle of the canvas of pale blue on top and almost black on the bottom. I watched in silent awe. Then I turned to the right and looked out of the window. It was completely dark. Nothingness stared back at me. I turned to the left again and the sunset was even more glorious.

There I was — on the same plane — the same person — looking at the same sky — but I needed to angle my head to the left to catch the beauty. I'm glad I didn't concentrate on the bleakness of the right side.

Maybe as we travel through life, what we must remember to do is just get a different perspective in order to be able to appreciate the beauty that surrounds us.

WE MISS OUT ON SO MUCH WHEN WE LOOK ONLY IN ONE DIRECTION.

BURN-OUT

Forget what you've heard about it. Concentrate more on not rusting-out which is infinitely more dangerous.

I encourage you to burn-out several times in your lifetime. It is something that happens only to those who live intensely. Although it is lonely, it is tolerable when we realize that the internal combustion system will be operating again at full speed once the discomfort of knowing we're ready for a change has been accepted. For many, it is the first step to letting go of the familiar.

Beware of rust-out. It is slow and insidious. If you want to know what it looks like, take a look at someone who has been on the job for twenty-four years and is just hanging in there to collect retirement. Or the ones whose marriage died years ago, but neither has had the courage to bury. Or if you're brave, look in the mirror. If the eyes say, "Where do I go from here?" REJOICE!

THAT PROBABLY MEANS YOU'RE GOING TO DO SOMETHING THAT WILL GET YOU THE RIGHT ANSWER.

RELIGION

Sometimes I meet people I have never seen before and my soul seems to speak to theirs immediately, and we make a connection that can only be described as the culmination of some unfinished business from long, long ago in another place and another time.

As you and I sit in our place of worship — mine is the beach — I wonder if maybe all of us aren't just a little wrong and also just a little right?

And if that is so, then what is all the fuss about?

SOMEWHERE, WE SEEM TO HAVE TAKEN A WRONG TURN. I THINK IT WAS AT THE CORNER OF DENOMINATIONALISM ROAD AND I'VE GOT THE ONLY ANSWER FOR EVERYONE AVENUE.

IF I HAD MY LIFE TO LIVE OVER . . . . .

I would never attend a committee meeting.

I'd hug my kids more and complain less about their messy room.

I'd sing more and cry less.

I'd marry the same man.
And I'd appreciate him long before I was middle-aged.

Feelings

PEACEFUL INSECURITY

There is great peace in knowing why you are on this earth.

It is not something that can be explained too much.

You know — and that is enough.

It is not imperative that others know or understand.

As long as it makes sense to you, all the other validations are irrelevant.

IF I KNOW THAT TO BE TRUE, HOW COME I STILL SOMETIMES WANT EVERYONE TO LOVE AND RESPECT AND UNDERSTAND ME?

IMAGE

DEFINITION: What we labor the most to fabricate while we lose our real selves in the process.

Can you imagine a consultant's advice to Eleanor Roosevelt? "Ellie Baby, you've got to develop a little charisma. Dump the dark colors and tacky hats. Let's get you a voice coach and see if we can't bring your high pitched sound down a little. People won't listen to what you have to say unless the voice is well modulated. And let's get you an appointment to straighten out the teeth, OK?"

Or to Jimmy Durante. "Hey, Jim, you're a talented guy but the world is full of piano players. First thing ya gotta do is get a nose job if you wanna make it in the movies, know what I mean?"

Or to Art Buchwald, who was on the program of a convention I worked at and left the people smiling, delighted and excited. "Artie, let's sign you up for one of those courses that will teach you how to dress for success. No frumpy suits for a man who wants to make it. Silk ties and custom made shirts are a must. And let's try some elocution lessons that'll help you lose that New York accent. Trust me. I know what works in this business."

HAVE YOU EVER NOTICED THAT PEOPLE WHO HAVE SOUL AND SUBSTANCE DON'T NEED TO CREATE AN IMAGE?
THEY JUST ARE.

17

THE OTHER SIDE OF THE COIN

Remember the movie where the characters said, "May the Force be with you"?
If I had been one of the writers, the line would have been, "May you be with the Force."

You see, I'm aware the Force is always with us. We are the ones who separate ourselves from It by our behavior, attitude, life style, lack of faith-hope-commitment, but all we have to do is reach out and get in touch with it. And when we really do that — regardless of what it is we do in life — the universe will seem to flow in the direction we most need it to at that moment.

Observe closely the people who struggle and climb over anyone and anything to attain what they want. Stick around long enough and see most of it eventually turn to dust.

Watch the ones who enjoy and share and dream with a dedication to something greater than themselves. See the ones who don't watch the clock but simply continue until the work is done. Watch the magical coincidences that bring the right people at the right time to their door. They receive an abundance of the very riches the others have pursued with such futile effort.

MAYBE THERE IS A LAW OF LIFE IN THERE SOME-WHERE WE HAVE CHOSEN TO IGNORE FOR TOO LONG. I IMAGINE IT JUST SOUNDS TOO SIMPLE TO BE TRUE.

PROGRAMMING

Have you ever picked up the phone and received news that altered your life forever? I have.

Until then, I set goals and had an inner time schedule for all I wanted to accomplish and how I would do it. Since then, I have learned quickly and painfully that our best laid plans are for naught. What meant so much to me yesterday will be totally unworthy of pursuit tomorrow if the jolt of today is powerful enough.

Ever since then, I stopped giving much thought to what I want happening in my life five or ten years from now. I concentrate on now and today and the person I'm with at the moment. Some years later I often look back and marvel at what has transpired in the interim, but it has all happened one day at a time.

DO I HAVE HOPES AND DREAMS FOR THE FUTURE? OF COURSE. BUT NOT AT THE EXPENSE OF TODAY.

PASSION

She says she would give anything to play guitar the way I do. I ask her, "Have you got half an hour? I'll teach you everything I know."

We both giggle.

But I know I've told her the truth. The short-order cook taught me six chords. Everything else they saw today was passion. Amazing what a little knowledge combined with a lot of passion will accomplish.

That's where the school system fails. Enthusiastic human beings go into universities and carbon copies come out many years later, mouthing phrases like, "That certainly seems like a viable alternative." Vital knowledge is not found in schools, and we must be courageous enough to know that and seek it elsewhere — including within ourselves. Why do we listen to Leo Buscaglia and find our hearts beating to the rhythm of yes-yes-yes-yes? Because he is expressing what we have known all along.

The problem is we've been conditioned to think that source lacks credibility and expertise.

If I have such strong feelings about the value of formal education, why have I spent so many years in schools? Because I also knew there was something very special I'd find there.

I REMEMBER SPECIAL HUMAN BEINGS WHO EN-RICHED ME BY THEIR PRESENCE AND STYLE AND DEDICATION LONG AFTER I HAD FORGOTTEN EVERYTHING THAT WAS IN THEIR BOOKS AND THE TERM PAPERS I TURNED IN TO THEM.

Children

THE COMPETITION

One of them played the piano.

The other played guitar.

The guests applauded.

The third one whispered, "Since I don't have a talent, do you want me to bring out the drawers from my room to show them how neat I am?" It was only then that I understood the belligerent look in her ten-year-old eyes.

How insensitive we adults are sometimes when we use our children to make us look good.

The strong ones don't play the game.

BRAVO!

WHAT YOU SEE IS WHAT YOU <u>DON'T</u> GET

"Aunt Wosie . . . you are UGLY in the morning, huh?"

She said the words so gently with what could only be described as pity. My niece had always seen me looking my best as I popped in during business trips, and this was the first time I had stayed overnight. As she stood there by the bed, her brother who was a few years older, blurted, "Shirley, Aunt Rosie is beautiful on the inside where it counts."

She screwed up her seven-year-old face and I could almost see the lightbulb go off in her blond head. Very gingerly, without a moment's hesitation, she lifted the covers and the sheet in order to search for the beautiful me *inside* where he said it was. I'm not sure she ever found it.

HOW ABOUT YOU? HAVE YOU LIFTED <u>YOUR</u> COVER LATELY?

HOMEWORK

She was crying and looking at me with disappointment in her big brown eyes. "You were better to talk to when you were just a Mommy. Now you're a social worker and you sit there and ask me how I feel about it — and that stinks! I wish you hadn't gone back to school. Before, you really cared. Your eyes used to talk to me and give me answers. Now your mouth does and I'm as confused as ever."

It has taken me ten years to un-learn much of what I've been taught. I was a much more effective, natural, people-person before I got the letters after my name.

THAT'S WHY I DON'T USE THEM.

THE LITTLE ACORN

It is possible that you, too, have a child who is not a scholar and is having difficulty in school. Ten years ago we sat with a little girl who cried because her grades were low, her spelling was atrocious, and her reading skills were two years behind her classmates. They recommended that she repeat a grade and she was humiliated.

We hugged her and told her she was extremely bright, even though that wasn't reflected on paper. We told her we loved her and wanted her to know that all we expected of her was that she do her best — whatever that was — without comparing herself to her sisters. We both knew there was a lot more to life than an "A" on a report card.

Today, she is in her first year of college. Her favorite subject is economics. In high school, she was captain of the cheerleading squad and co-editor of the award-winning yearbook. She was on the Homecoming Court and her scrapbooks are full of honors bestowed upon her over the years. When she was asked to write why she felt she deserved to be the Senior of Distinction her classmates and teachers had voted her to be, she wrote that although she wasn't a brilliant student, she had learned a lot about working with what she had, instead of worrying about what she lacked, and the value of enthusiasm, determination, and having fun along the way.

For some reason, I sit here typing and crying.

WE'VE MADE A LOT OF MISTAKES AS PARENTS, BUT WHEN I'M MOST DISCOURAGED, I REMEMBER THE FEW THINGS WE SEEM TO HAVE DONE RIGHT, AND THAT SUSTAINS ME.

THE TWIG AND THE TREE

Her boyfriend had behaved badly and now her feelings were hurt and I hurt for her, too.
Within hours, she called to invite him to a movie.
"Movie!" I ranted. "Let him stew in his own juice for awhile. Let him suffer a little."

She looked at me with steely determination in her eyes.

"You always told me a relationship takes a lot of work. Why does anyone have to suffer anymore today? He knows he was a jerk and I know he was a jerk, but he's also a lot more than that."

She drove off and I smiled.

She had learned the lesson too well.

I'M THE ONE WHO NEEDED A REFRESHER COURSE.

THE LAW OF GRAVITY

In the sixties when other young women were burning their bras, the most I did was walk around the house in my muu-muu without one. I quit that the day one of the kids said I reminded her of the natives pictured in *National Geographic.*

Today, they are nineteen, twenty-two and twenty-four and I am aware of how envious I am of their firm bodies and taut skin. I think it all began when the eldest was six and asked if someday her legs, too, would have some Very Close Veins.

I FEEL LIKE THE HUNDRED-YEAR-OLD MAN IN THE JOKE WHO LAMENTED, "IF I'D KNOWN I WAS GO-ING TO LIVE THIS LONG, I WOULD HAVE TAKEN BETTER CARE OF MYSELF."

PRIORITIES

Although we may all be sharing the same earth, only a space-case could believe it is the same world for all people.

A group of children were seated on the floor of the After School House and our project for the day was to make something from pieces of fabric that had been donated. As I planned the afternoon activity, I envisioned making doll clothes or pot holders.

Two little girls grabbed most of the fabric and would not let go. They both wanted to make a pillow and needed lots of stuffing for it. It seems there were so many people living in their apartment, the only ones who had their own pillow and bed were the adults. Their behavior with those scraps was desperate, pushy and obstinate.

I UNDERSTOOD, THOUGH. WHEN YOUR HIER-ARCHY OF NEEDS IS AT SUCH A BASIC LEVEL, GOOD MANNERS DON'T SEEM VERY IMPORTANT.

Pets

OF LICE AND MEN

I've always thought people who made a big fuss about their animals were ridiculous.

Then we got Rocky and that beautiful, noble dog lived with us for fourteen years and now my opinion is different. There isn't a time I see a German Shepherd I don't think of her and miss her and get a lump in my throat. I wish I hadn't worried so much about her shedding in my clean house.

We do so much talking and planning about sweeping social reforms. Files bulge with notes and recommendations for correcting society's ills. Maybe it will happen on an individual basis—just as it did with Rocky and me. I love dogs now. I wonder why I'm comparing people to dogs?

PERHAPS BECAUSE I FEEL WE COULD LEARN A LOT FROM THEM.

CONDITIONING

She was just a mutt and would never take Rocky's place. I let her know that from the beginning. I fed her and put fresh water in her dish but that was about it. One day she would not eat. Or the second. Or the third. I patted her and stroked her and asked her what was wrong. The caring in my voice surprised me. She gobbled up the food, drank the water, and wagged her tail. Weeks later I was convinced it was a coincidence based on other variables. She could have been ill. (I was taught to be objective in school.)

So I just put the food out without petting her first. By the second day of not eating, the experiment was complete and I needed no other proof.

If a pat on the head can mean that much to a dog, can you imagine what a hug must mean to a child?

"Yeah" you say, "but I didn't get them."

Go out there and get them now! The world is full of huggers. How will you recognize them? Hold out your arms.

AND IF THEY DON'T RECIPROCATE, DON'T ASSUME THEY ARE NOT HUGGERS. THEY MAY BE HURTING SO MUCH AT THAT MOMENT THAT SUCH A DE-GREE OF INTIMACY IS MORE THAN THEY CAN HANDLE. LET THEM KNOW WITH YOUR EYES, YOU'LL STILL BE AVAILABLE WITH YOUR HUGS WHEN THEY ARE READY.

VERY OLD SPICE

He was nineteen and I was eighteen and he always smelled of Old Spice aftershave lotion and wore white shirts with the sleeves rolled up. He was my first sweetheart and the first man with whom I ever experienced tender moments. He went away to the Air Force and taped my picture on his locker door — the one where I was looking coquettishly at the camera and showing off the tiny waistline. I kept his photo under the glass top of the desk at the bank where I worked, and I bragged to anyone who would listen about how great he was.

I don't brag to others now. I tell him. He is approaching fifty and looks tired, and is fatter. So am I. We sit in the same room for hours and don't say much, though sometimes we look at each other for a long time, smiling silently. And I could almost swear his eyes see a coquette with a tiny waist.

Neither of us is beyond temptation. The world is full of other desirable people. We've just privately decided the price would be too much to pay.

IF THERE IS ANY FEELING THAT COMPARES WITH BEING THE LOVE IN THE RIGHT PERSON'S EYES — I HAVEN'T EXPERIENCED IT.

REALITY VS. THE MEDIA

Many of our friends are on their second and third marriages. Sometimes, they ask me what our "secret" is. Did we love each other more? I doubt it. There were many times when we hated each other. Fifteen years ago, Jimmy the Greek would have bet you this union would not endure. Maybe what made the difference was compassion. I understood why he might be acting less than wonderful, and he continued to love me when I was most unlovable. We seem to have emerged from all the bad times liking each other a little better because that is when we really got to know each other. The bond became stronger and loyalty developed.

Still, this is not the way I expected it to be. Where are the flowers? The furs? The jewelry? The elegance? (His idea of dressing for dinner is to put on a clean T-shirt!)

Those ads with those chic people may be doing us a great injustice. It's difficult to capture a warm hug, or proud look, or hearty laugh on paper, for when all is said and done, maybe that's all love is.

THE REST MAY BE JUST HYPE.

CREATIVE PROBLEM SOLVING

The set was blaring, "Heeeeere's Johnny!" and he was whispering sweet nothings in my ear.

I looked at him with the disdain that only a wife of over twenty years would dare display and said in my firmest voice, "Please, I want to watch the Carson show. Burt Reynolds is on tonight."

He didn't say a word. He walked to the TV set, turned it off, stood in front of it with arms and legs outstretched and murmured in his best Humphrey Bogart voice, "Burt Reynolds ain't all that's on tonight, Baby. Would you settle for the Original Amateur Hour?"

I did.

EAT YOUR HEART OUT, BURT.

I'M FOR MEN'S LIB

Now that he has worked for over twenty-five years, I'm looking forward to having him relax in his workshop while I bring home the check. But not like the gal on TV who claims to bring home the bacon, fry it up in a pan, always has every hair in place, doesn't perspire, and never lets him forget he's a man.

If truth be told, on days when I come home from doing my thing, I'm either too exhausted or elated to want to remind Robert Redford that he's a man, much less the chubby guy who's walking around scratching and asking if he's got clean socks. I need nurturing, too. The kind of equality I'd like to see in our marriage is an acceptance of options, so we are both sharing all aspects of the marriage relationship.

TRANSLATION: I'M WAITING FOR THE DAY WHEN HE DEALS WITH THE RING AROUND THE COLLAR AND THE TY-D-BOL MAN FOR A CHANGE.

ANGER

As his plane took off, I fantasized about what a Merry Widow I would be when it crashed and he died in it. I was so angry at him!

Months later the guilt was bothering me and I confessed my deep, dark, terrible thoughts. He was very quiet. Finally he said, "I'll tell you the truth, Babes. In all the years I've known you, no matter how angry I got with you, I never wished you would die in a plane crash. A case of terminal beri-beri — yes. A slow, deliberate murder — absolutely. But never a plane crash."

THERE ARE THOSE WHO WONDER WHAT I SEE IN HIM, INCLUDING ME SOMETIMES. AND THEN AT TIMES LIKE THOSE I KNOW.

Work

THE SEARCH

If what you're doing in your work is an expression and extension of who and what you are as a person, my guess is you would do it even if you didn't get paid for it. Or did it for many years until you were.

That's how I feel about my work. I searched long and dug deep. Without prior planning, I found me along the way. I didn't even know that's what I was looking for.

I find seeing work as an extension of self to be a universal feeling among people who love their jobs. Years ago I recognized that same commitment to excellence in the woman who helped me clean house a few times a month. She was enamored of what she did.

Give unending thanks if you have found something like that in your life. And keep searching if you haven't. Just because you haven't come across it doesn't mean it isn't out there waiting for you to discover it. Or more accurately — waiting for you to relax long enough so it can find <u>you</u>.

This book began twenty years ago when the kids would do or say something I wanted to remember and I started to put little notes into a file labeled, "Kid's Unforgettables." Six years ago I typed a really terrible manuscript with some of these thoughts. I put it all on a back burner and decided to wait until my inner clock said "Go" again.

YOU, TOO, HAVE A BOOK, OR A SONG, OR AN INVENTION, OR A BUSINESS VENTURE IN YOU. WHEN WILL YOU TURN IT INTO A REALITY?

DISTRACTIONS

My peripheral vision caught sight of a man in the front row unzipping his pants. It was a Saturday afternoon and I was sharing my music with mental patients in a state mental hospital. The people were medicated, lethargic, and, for the most part, disinterested. Always, however, I could spot one pair of eyes with whom the music was really making contact, and it was for that one person that I was there.

It became increasingly difficult for me to continue singing as if nothing were happening. My eyes were being diverted and I was uneasy not only with my embarrassment but with my curiosity. I searched the room for staff to rescue me. No such luck. The psychologist sat there with a look that said, "It's not my problem."

One of the patients showed more empathy than the professional. She picked up my discomfort and said, "Never mind him. He always does that." ALWAYS? "Not in front of me!" I thought. Ignoring the behavior had obviously not extinguished it. What he was doing wasn't crazy, but I thought it was insane to consider it acceptable behavior in front of forty other people. If he were outside this ward, someone would say something to indicate their disapproval. That's the day I learned that the craziest thing at a mental institution is often the attitude of the sane people.

I looked him straight in the eye, not an easy thing to do under the circumstances, and told him that while I was playing guitar that was not to be done. I asked him to leave the room if he wished to continue. Without a word, he zipped his pants and I continued singing. I could almost swear there was a look in his eyes that said, "I was wondering when someone would notice me."

Years later, I called a hospital to inquire about the condition of a friend who had just come out of surgery. Can you understand why, when the voice at the other end said, "The patient is holding his own" I laughed so hard I had to hang up quickly?

I OFTEN LAUGH LOUDEST WHEN I'M MOST UNCOMFORTABLE WITH MY THOUGHTS.

PAYMENT DUE

The doctor charges me $135.00 for the fifteen minutes I spend in his office and I resent it. Then I think of what my honorarium is for a one hour program and I realize that sometimes what we get for the work we perform today is actually payment for what we went through yesterday that prepared us for the services we are now able to render. My "hour" took twelve years of work and experimentation and giving the music away. Under a tree in a migrant labor camp while the workers sang their Mexican songs with me. On the floor of the psycho-social rehabilitation center in a room full of people who were, for the most part, lost in their own world. In the school with the retarded kids who responded instinctively and joyously to what the music was communicating. Sometimes I feel I'm being awarded compensation for that afternoon at the mental hospital. I considered giving up on my dream of using music for something other than entertainment that day. Only my sense of humor helped me get through that humiliating experience.

I don't think we give enough importance to the value of humor in our lives. That may be one of the traits that separates winners from losers. Norman Cousins relates that it helped him overcome a debilitating disease. I believe it. It is interesting how much humorous material has come from devastating moments in my life. That fascinates me. It is almost as if some of us vow: "I will not allow life to vanquish me. I will find something in this that I will use constructively and go on — laughing."

WHAT HAPPENS TO PEOPLE WHO DON'T HAVE THAT COPING MECHANISM?

THE DO-GOODERS

The Girl Scout troop was immaculately groomed in their uniforms with white gloves and sashes full of badges. We were to deliver a Thanksgiving basket to a needy family and the excitement of our good deed was invigorating as we drove, singing happy songs, to the other side of town, across the railroad tracks.

When we arrived, the door was cracked open with apprehension and confusion. A woman seated at a metal-topped table was holding a baby while the older children peeked from behind her, staring at the eager group congregated at her front door. She didn't react as we had expected. She hissed with old anger. "I cain't cook that bird. We don't have no gas. They shut it off yestiddy. I don't have a pan big enough for that thing." Behind the old, bitter, tired look I saw pride and dignity in eyes that accused, "How could you do this in front of my children? And the neighbors! They saw you bring food to us!"

That was the day I decided that the only thing worse than ignoring the plight of those in need is misdirected charity that produces a euphoric high in the giver at the expense of the humiliation of the receiver. Ever since then, if I'm about to so something charitable that can be written into minutes or reported by someone at a meeting, I run in the other direction.

Once again, I changed on that day. That evening, when one of our daughters was complaining because she had to wait to get into one of the three bathrooms, I sat on the floor and cried. The girls were very small then and they seemed puzzled that I would be so upset about something so foolish. I was too emotionally drained to bother explaining.

BESIDES, I'M NOT SURE KIDS WHO GET VIDEO CASSETTE GAMES FOR CHRISTMAS INSTEAD OF A NEW PAIR OF SHOES WOULD UNDERSTAND. BE HONEST. HOW WOULD YOUR KIDS REACT IF THEY FOUND AN ORANGE IN THEIR CHRISTMAS STOCKING?

LET'S PRETEND

The task was to write a paper on public assistance and I thought that rather than go to the libraries, I would stand in line at a local office and go through the machinations necessary to apply for food stamps. It was "on the job training" and I felt like a reporter.

I arrived very early and already the lines were forming in front of the building. When the doors opened there was a rush to obtain a number. For five and a half hours I sat there observing. I was a student and this was simply research for a term paper, though I pretended to be one of "them."

That was the day I learned that but for the grace of God, "them" is "me."

Something happened to me that day. I left there feeling a lot less secure and confident. The little old lady told me her husband had been a contractor, had suffered an illness that wiped out their savings and business, and was now doing something she never dreamed she'd ever do: asking for help in order to eat.

I realized why so many people there had such a dead look in their eyes. It was an insensitive game for me to play.

THAT DAY, I BECAME A LITTLE LESS THAN WHAT I THOUGHT I WAS CAPABLE OF BEING. NO PAPER AND NO GRADE IS WORTH INTRUDING SURREPTITIOUSLY INTO ANOTHER'S PRIVATE PAIN.

LEGACY

It is late at night and he calls from New York and there is excitement in his voice. He confirms my speaking engagement now that he has heard a tape and I thank him for his enthusiasm. It comes across the telephone and embraces me.

He confesses, "All I know, Rosita, is that after I heard it, I wanted to come home and hug my wife."

Years ago if you had asked me what I hoped to accomplish with my work, I would have given you grandiose concepts. Today, I am thrilled that it is something so simple. Perhaps all I will ever contribute to this world is a song and a few hugs.

THE MIRACLE TO ME IS THAT TODAY THAT SEEMS LIKE MORE THAN ENOUGH.

GOAL SETTING

Success-oriented executives accustomed to long term goal setting often flinch when I suggest living life spontaneously, being ready to accept whatever the moment brings and making instant decisions based on a gut feeling.

I understand their need for specifics, but I will not change my programs to fit their preconceptions. If I'm going to worry about having everyone agree with me, I am rendered incapable of giving a mental health message with my songs.

They sit there with pens and papers poised, and when I ask them to put all of that away, I sense the resistance. I remind them that most of the notes taken will be stuffed in a notebook or folder and filed at home or in the office, never to be looked at again. Ah — then they laugh because they know I've done the same thing, too.

When I begin to have them experience the moment, they sometimes squirm uncomfortably. Until later.
Later, they smile and reach out to one another and something special happens that none of us can describe very well but we can feel it intensely. A woman once wrote, "I just suddenly felt happier to be alive, although I'm not sure what IT is you taught me."

IF THAT IS WHAT SHE LEFT WITH, I'M NOT SURE IT IS IMPORTANT.

PERFECTIONISM

"If a thing is worth doing, it's worth doing badly—at first."

I heard Jim Newman, author of <u>Release Your Brakes!</u> say that from the platform one day and I sat there in the audience silently shouting YES! YES! YES! It was one of those "Ah-ha!" experiences that suddenly confirm something we've known but had not conceptualized until someone or something served as a catalyst for understanding it. It doesn't matter that the thought may have been around a long time. It was the first time I had heard it, so to me it was new and exciting. Although I was not scheduled to speak until five hours after Jim, I went out of my way to be there for his session that morning because I had a feeling he might say one thing that I really needed to hear.

Do you remember the first time you drove a car? Can you recall tying your first shoe lace or planning your first dinner party? Were you as adept at starting a lawnmower the first time? Could you sit down at the typewriter and not look at the keys? The point is, many of us have been taught, "If you're not going to do it right, don't do it at all." If I had followed that advice, I never would have picked up the guitar the second time. What was so awkward twenty years ago, now feels like an extension of my arm.

IF I WERE RAISING KIDS TODAY, I'D REMEMBER TO REPEAT JIM'S PHRASE TO THEM OFTEN. I HAVE A FEELING WE COULD RAISE A DYNAMITE GENERATION OF HUMAN BEINGS.

THE INTERNAL BAROMETER

Have you ever sat in an audience and seen or heard something or someone that caused a tingling in your spine and goose bumps on your arms? Those are the indicators I wish we had when reading about someone's work by studying their curriculum vitae.

I remember the speaker when I graduated from college. His credentials took up almost two pages on the program. He listed every committee and club he belonged to. Within five minutes I knew that guy had nothing to say I wanted or needed to hear.

Maybe that is why, when I have been asked to participate in a panel presentation about the use of music for something other than entertainment, I've declined.

Don't ask me to talk about music.

Or creativity.

Or joy.

Let me share it with you and then you will know.
And if after that, you don't, all the explanations I could have given would have been worthless.

WHEN WILL WE ACCEPT THAT SOME THINGS ARE NOT TRANSLATABLE INTO WORDS?

WHO'S WHO?

The envelope was postmarked England and I was surprised and delighted to find that I was to be included in an <u>International Who's Who of Women.</u> I had always wondered how that was done!

Then I read further. They wanted a bio and a photo. There was no charge for this; however, if I wanted to receive a copy of the book, I was to mail a check for $62.60, and if I wanted the deluxe leather-bound edition, the price was considerably more.

My ego wanted me to reply. My soul encouraged me to tear the letter up and discard it. I realized how often we fill our lives with empty honors. We display them on our ego walls. Then one day, someone lowers our body six feet into the ground, or scatters our ashes and someone takes everything off the wall and puts it into a box for awhile. Years later, they eventually throw it all away. You see, what people will remember about us is our smile. Or the way we cooked lasagna. Or how they could depend on us. Or how we believed in them when no one else did. Or how clever we were about fixing mechanical things. Twenty years later they will comment, "Boy! If Gerry were here, he'd know how to do this!" I doubt if many will say, "Do you remember that forty thousand dollar car he drove?"

We keep awards in our family that have value. One of them is a piece of leather on which three little girls, who didn't have money to buy a Father's Day gift, wrote how they felt about their daddy. And it ended like this, "You always say that parents have never been parents before and if they make mistakes it's because they don't know any better. They are just using their common sence (sic). Now either you have great common sence, Dad, or terrific beginner's luck!"

ARE YOU SELECTIVE ABOUT THE AWARDS YOU WORK FOR, AND KEEP AND CHERISH?

Strengths ~ Inadequacies ~ Strengths ~ Inadequacies

SUCCESS

When I was hung up on not failing, I accomplished very little. It was necessary for me to fail at many things before I could sort out what it was that really mattered. Success begins in the head. Long before I was doing what I'm doing today, I envisioned it all in my mind, although I didn't have the vaguest idea what steps I needed to take to arrive here. I played it by ear. Some would call that creative visualization. Others would label it self-fulfilling prophecy. I prefer to think of it as the art of waste disposal.

When we work at discarding a great deal of excess along the way, we are left only with a small concentrated essence instead of watered-down quantities. Then we can devote our energies to do what Thoreau suggested — "advance confidently in the direction of our dreams."

Even so, years later we may look back incredulously and wonder, "Did I do THAT?"

Morley has written, "There is only one success. To live your own life in your own way."

TO THAT I WOULD ADD, "AND TO DO IT IN SUCH A WAY THAT THE MOST SKILLED MORTICIAN WILL HAVE A TOUGH TIME WIPING THE GRIN FROM YOUR FACE."

I DON'T KNOW WHAT I WANT TO BE WHEN I GROW UP

When said by a child, that statement is met with understanding and a sympathetic smile. When expressed by a forty, fifty, or sixty-year-old, panic prevails. It takes courage to change. And sometimes desperation, too. When our comfort zone is determined by the paycheck we receive every two weeks, the car we drive, the dimensions of our office, or the peer group we socialize with, it is difficult to consider putting some of those aside in anticipation of other kinds of riches that are not as visible to the eye.

Often, we are identified and validated according to our position. When filling out an application for credit, I was perceived and treated differently when I wrote that I was an Associate Director of a Mental Health Association than now when I say that I am a Musical Communicator at conventions and meetings.

The fact that I do more effective social work with a guitar than I was ever capable of doing from behind a desk is of little consequence to others. Titles give messages. So that is why when you and I make changes in our lives that make sense to us, one of the first security blankets we must discard is our definition of self according to societal values.

For years I did "important" work that enabled me to make a living. One day I decided to just go wherever my music led me. My friends thought I had accepted a better paying position elsewhere. Actually, I sat home for eight months, did a lot of soul searching and ultimately developed the business that now brings me such joy.

One year after walking out of the office, I had eliminated all but sixteen names and phone numbers from the bulging Rolodex file I thought I could not get through a day without. Today, I earn in one hour what I was paid for working 40-50 hours a week for six weeks. Same woman. Same talents. Same strengths but same weaknesses also.

WHAT MADE THE DIFFERENCE? I DECIDED IT WAS POSSIBLE, WITH GOD'S HELP. AND SO IT WAS.

ORGIES

For some, that word conjures up images of the Roman Empire and maidens feeding grapes to men reclining on the floor in their togas.

It reminds me of Oreos.

And if you don't know what an Oreo is, you're probably reading the wrong book. Grab the nearest copy of "Getting High On Sprouts" and you will probably benefit more.

An Oreo Orgy takes place when the milk turns grey and the dunking fingers get "pruney." At no time do the number of Oreos and the amount of milk in the glass ever come out even. When you have cookies left over, you run out of milk; when you have enough milk, you have no cookies.

THAT'S LIFE. WE SELDOM HAVE ENOUGH---OF THE THINGS THAT MATTER THE LEAST.

CHARACTER

Are you an employer considering me for a job? Don't bother administering a lie detector test. Just leave me in a room with a Sara Lee pound cake for twenty minutes. You'll know everything about my character you need to know when you re-enter the room and see me brushing the crumbs away.

A bag of cookies is another dilemma. The cookie jar is never large enough to hold the entire bag. What do thin people do at times like that? Surely they, too, must eat all the broken ones to make space. But they have some magic gene in them that does not permit them to gain weight.

For most of my life I have failed my own will power test. It is conducted every time I come home with groceries. I'm beginning to think it is an exercise in masochism to continue setting myself up for failure. Maybe I'll buy a larger cookie jar.

BUT IF I DO THAT, WHAT WILL MY EXCUSE BE FOR EATING ALL THE BROKEN ONES?

FEAR

It doesn't go away completely.

I still feel it when I walk into a party where I don't know anyone. And I have to do deep breathing exercises when I get on a plane. And I feel a knot in my stomach when our daughters look at me the way I used to look at Mama so long ago — when I thought she was from outer space because her views were so alien to mine.

But when I most expect it, fear isn't there. It takes a vacation. It is replaced by strength that comes from a place where it seems to have been stored for a long time. I followed Dr. Norman Vincent Peale on the platform one memorable night and walked out relaxed and had the time of my life in front of 2,600 people. Where was fear then?

I don't understand fear any better now than I did when I was a kid, except that today my songs seem to give me courage.

PLEASE, GOD, DON'T LET THAT MEAN I HAVE TO GO THROUGH LIFE WITH A GUITAR STRAPPED ON MY BACK.

THE DESERT ISLAND

Years ago, if you had asked who I'd like to be stranded on a desert island with, my list would have included lots of famous men.

If I were making that list today, most of them would be women. Dynamic human beings like Maya Angelou, Erma Bombeck, Dinah Shore, my brilliant and witty friend, Carole.

What I've just written is of interest only to me. I've done that in order to get you to think about it, too, because your answers today may be a pretty good indication of how you've changed.

I'm not sure what this change means, but I suspect that the more I accepted and loved myself, the easier it became for me to see and appreciate the wonderful qualities in other women, too.

Who would the men on my list be? Not my husband, Ray. After all, we are talking fantasy here, and he is very much a reality. One guy would be Gary Collins, the host on HOUR MAGAZINE and the other would be John Denver.

AND TOM SELLECK WOULD VISIT ON WEEKENDS.

PAWNS

Consider for a moment what our lives would be like without needing to account to the IRS. We would take someone to lunch because we really wanted to be with them and pay cash and not ask for a receipt. The people we love, and the good times we have with them would not be tax deductions. We wouldn't keep a log of our mileage. We'd purchase property because we fell in love with it instead of reasoning that it promised to be a good return on our investment.

I long for the simple life. In my own way, sometimes I attain it.

Our CPA was appalled when we said we bought the old beach house because the view of the Gulf and the sunsets were the most magnificent on the island.
"But you could have invested that money in multiple rental units or a tax shelter!" His usually delightful smile was replaced by disbelief at our naiveté.

It's tough to explain to a CPA that you're a dreamer.

If you are, too, please hold on tenaciously to that impractical part of you.

Don't lose it along the way.

IN THE LONG RUN, IT MAY BE THE ONLY MEANINGFUL LONG-RANGE INVESTMENT YOU MAKE.

ASSUMPTIONS

They assume that because they have seen me working with such ease and joy, the same competency displayed spills over into all areas of my life. Obviously, they weren't in the audience when I first started and had to take sips of water between sentences because the dry mouth felt like I had swallowed a box of cotton balls covered with peanut butter. I'm so glad I didn't give up and did hang in there until it all became such fun. I knew it would, eventually!

If these people who make assumptions would speak to the lady at the bank, they'd know the rest of the story. Every year and a half or so, she opens a new checking account for me because I can't make heads or tails of the mess of figures I'm confronted with. I solve it by starting anew with a fresh balance, different color checks, and another account number. If the old account remains dormant long enough, it straightens itself out. My friend, the one who is a bookkeeper, says that is a ridiculous solution and seems quite distressed that an intelligent woman would allow herself the luxury of such a streak of plain dumb.

I wish she'd get off my back. It has taken me a lifetime to admit there are some things I'm incompetent doing, and I'm enjoying it. I've just recently learned how to give up. I know the freedom of no longer trying beyond a certain point. When I do too much trying, I know I'm already failing. It may seem sophomoric to handle an account reconciliation in such a manner, but if I devoted days to those little numbers and to getting the balance just right, I would be regressing. I shared that thought at a program I did for a group of bankers and a lady in the audience whispered, "Thank you. I've been doing that for years, but I thought I was the only one!"

HEY PEOPLE — YOU'RE TALKIN' TO A WOMAN WHO SETS THE RECORD FOR RUNNING THE MILE WHEN THE BANK STATEMENT ARRIVES AT THE SAME TIME THE HUSBAND PULLS INTO THE DRIVEWAY . .

A STAR IS <u>NOT</u> BORN

I look at Streisand on the screen and she looks terrific in her frizzy natural hairdo.

The next day I walk into the beauty salon and ask the man to cut mine the same way.

I envision looking good enough to tempt Alan Alda into leaving his wife for me.

I leave the shop looking like a brunette Phyllis Diller after sticking her finger in a light socket.

SO MUCH FOR MY FANTASIES.

MRS. CLEAN

When I was growing up, the greatest compliment a woman in our social circle could be paid was to say she was so clean, you could eat off her floors.

I tried. I really tried. Through all the years of little kids with spilled milk and dirty little fingerprints thirty inches off the floor all the way down the hall, I tried.

Then one day I stopped folding the towels in the linen closet exactly the same way. And that led to leaving newspapers and shoes in the living room overnight. And eventually the dishes waited until I really felt like doing them.

Doesn't sound like much, does it? Well, I know a lady who asks people to remove their shoes so her floors won't show scuff marks. And another soaks the switch-plates when she does housecleaning. And another insists her son drain the water in his waterbed every few months in order to "freshen" it.

How am I doing today? Can you eat off my floors?

YES. ASK ANY ANT OR COCKROACH IN THE HOUSE.

Sorrow

THE PSYCHOLOGIST

My daughter handed me a tissue as I flipped through the photo album and asked, "Why do you still cry when you look at pictures of Grandma, Mommy?"

In a moment of rare honesty I said to the child, "Because she died and I never sat down and really told her how much I loved her and how I knew she loved me — no matter how often we seemed not to appreciate each other."

She was very silent for a long time. I went on to other things. Then she asked, "Mommy, do you think I love you?" I answered distractedly, "Of course I do. Why?"

"How do you know? I never really sit down to tell you."

"Because when two people really love each other, each one of them knows it. You don't have to sit . . . ."

Thank you, doctor. Since that day I've been able to look at Mama's picture without crying. I wonder if other mothers give as much importance to what their kids are saying as they do to the celebrity shrinks on TV?

THE KIDS MAY HAVE A LOT MORE TO OFFER.

HOBBIES

The crewel picture measures two feet by three feet and takes up half of the wall over the piano. To everyone else it looks like an example of my needlework. I know it was "grief work."

In the months after she died I had to keep busy, so I spilled my tears onto a linen canvas combined with needle and thread and something magical happened: a lot of my sorrow stayed in that piece of fabric. It is so beautiful and brings me such joy today. Who would have thought it? Kahlil Gibran would have understood. In The Prophet he wrote that our joys spring forth from the same well that held our sorrows. Now I know what he meant.

We give too much importance to the finished products of our hobbies. The value of them in our lives is the purpose they serve at the time we're involved in them, not afterwards. That's why Ray will spend days working in the garage with his shop equipment and end up making sawdust.

WE WIVES NEED TO UNDERSTAND THAT SO WE'LL STOP ASKING THEM WHEN THE LAMP IS GOING TO BE FINISHED.

THE EXISTENTIAL MOMENT

You and I may need to sit and grieve over our own death before we live abundantly. Until I got in touch with the absolute, irrevocable reality that one day I would not be around to sing my songs, scratch my husband's back, and hug my kids, I kept postponing my life until tomorrow, when circumstances would be more perfect.

I stared at the embroideries on the wall that were evidence of twelve years of developing a hobby of mine. I looked at the table my husband made for the family room. I admired the ceramic Madonna our daughter had painted. And I cried. For the first time I really understood that one day I would not be here, in this form, to experience all this. And after the tears, came relief.

I became more enamored of life. Special people and special moments became more treasured. I stopped taking life for granted, and in so doing, I was able to make some important decisions about how I would spend the rest of my days. Once I put aside what it was I thought others expected of me, the choices were clear and easy. I wonder if others come to the same conclusions without going through the tears and confusion to get there?

And how many women reading this are now thinking I set Women's Lib back fifty years with my comment about scratching my husband's back?
What they don't know is that he scratches mine, too.

It fascinates me to think that I am keynoting at conventions that until recently had been a man's domain, unless you were a woman who had attained celebrity status. I am not a cute, young, perky, slim celebrity. I come from a minority culture. I have not achieved some great notoriety or fame. Why is it that nothing seems to be holding me back today from self-actualizing? Surely, soem would have predicted failure based on the facts.

BECAUSE I LEARNED RECENTLY THAT THE ONLY LIBERATION I NEED IS THE ONE I GRANT MYSELF. ONCE THAT IS DONE, THERE ARE NO BARRIERS.

FUNERALS

The older I get, the more of them I attend.
The more I attend, the less I feel.
The less I feel, the less I cry.

And when I do cry, it has little to do with the fact that
they died.

Mostly, I cry when I know they never really lived.
They had expired twenty years before the funeral.

OH YES. THEN I CRY A LOT.

DREAMS AND NIGHTMARES

If someone you've cared about has died, perhaps you've wondered about the fact that you don't seem to dream about them very often.   I would expect that a loss would trigger subconcious thoughts that would find expression in dreams.   I am now convinced that the number of times you dream about that person is not important.   What matters is that when it does happen, you get a message that will help you continue to live with acceptance of what cannot be changed.

Since Papa died, I've only dreamed about him once. The phone rings, and I hear his voice saying, "Rose . . . Rose?" and I become hysterical with joy and shout, "Papa! Papa! I thought you were dead!"

And his voice continues to drone, "Rose . . . Rose?" and I am in a panic as I realize that I can hear him, but he cannot hear me, so I jiggle the phone and speak louder and more distinctly in order to remedy the situation. And the voice at the other end continues to say, "Hello . . . Rose?"

Finally, I hang up because I know the wires are crossed, and no amount of effort on my part will correct the problem or make the other party hear me.

Somehow that bizarre dream calms me.   And gives me answers I've been searching for an entire lifetime.   Can you imagine a dream having that much importance? Why am I telling you something so personal when my inclination is to tear this sheet up? Because I want you to know you are not alone.   These are exactly the feelings we don't discuss with others, and we walk around feeling we are the only ones experiencing them. Often, I can't figure life out either.   And the longer I live the more I know that isn't what we're supposed to do, anyhow.

HOW ABOUT BOTH OF US DOING WHAT THE SONG ADVISES? "LET IT BE."

THE EYES HAVE IT

I never really saw the face of sorrow and grief until I saw it reflected in my sister-in-law's eyes when her baby died.

At the time it happened, I was out of town and Diana was babysitting with our three daughters. In eighteen years of marriage, it was the first time we had left the kids to vacation by ourselves and I was elated at the prospect. One day after I arrived in California from Florida, I dreamed that I was carrying a dead baby. I awoke crying hysterically and my husband could not calm me. It was a baby boy and in the nightmare I was inconsolable, as were the people who surrounded me. As the day went by, I couldn't shake the dream. I felt inexplicable sorrow. My husband, who recognizes my flair for the dramatic, suggested I felt guilty about having left the girls and told me to call home to assure myself that everything was all right. When I called, they told me Diana's little baby boy, born the day before, had died. They had not planned to tell us until we returned. There was nothing we could do, so why burden us with their sorrow so many miles away? The funeral was being held that day.

When I sat with Diana and we spoke of it later, her eyes were glazed and glassy. They had turned a vacant grey and seemed to reach to infinity. Her grief was so profound that I said little. I just sat there. Seldom have I felt more inadequate.

I never really saw the face of sorrow and grief until I saw it reflected in my sister-in-law's eyes. And I shall never forget what it looked like. Even as I type this, I find myself gasping.

THERE ARE LOSSES THAT HAVE NO WORDS. WE SURVIVE THEM, BUT WE KNOW WE ARE NO LONGER THE SAME PERSON WE WERE BEFORE.

COINCIDENCES

He has only one superstition.
He won't have anything to do with the number 13.
He moves into an apartment building that does not have a 13th floor.
He will not conduct business or travel on the 13th of the month.
And Tuesday is his least favorite day of the week.

He died on a Tuesday.
And when he was cremated, the three identification numbers on the little cardboard box added up to 13.

NO ONE ELSE NOTICED THAT. I DID. I AM CHANGED FOREVER.

I SAID IT COULDN'T BE DONE

"Come out, Mom! You have to see this!"
I hesitate. Nothing could be that important. I'm very busy.
I'm frying potatoes.

But they insist, so I reluctantly go outside and find that stretched across the sky, seemingly reaching from one end of the city to the other, is the most magnificent rainbow I have ever seen. We squeal. And express our sense of wonder out loud, accompanied by lots of pointing. We run around the block calling the other kids outside to see this outrageous display that Nature is offering.

The eldest goes inside to get her camera and I warn her that it is much too expansive a scene to capture with an Instamatic. She ignores me.

Years later while looking through an old photo album, I come across an incredible picture of a rainbow, and I remember that day.

She got the entire thing by shooting four pictures and combining them perfectly — but she never showed it to me. After all, I said it couldn't be done.

IT IS SO ENRICHING TO BE PROVED WRONG.

IMPRINTING

When they were very small, he would gather the three kids in his arms and snuggle his head into the crook of their neck and sniff around as he asked each one individually, "Is <u>this</u> my puppy? Is this <u>my</u> puppy? Is this my <u>puppy</u>?" And they would giggle with glee and squeal in affirmation that he had indeed found the right litter.

Fifteen years later, one of the girls came home from college to visit and he was sitting in front of the TV with that glazed look men get when things have not gone well at work that day. She sat on his lap, sniffed around his beard and ear and neck and said in her little girl voice, "Is <u>this</u> my Daddy? Is this <u>my</u> Daddy? Is this my <u>Daddy</u>?"

I witnessed an immediate transformation. Gone were the years and tiredness as he broke into a nostalgic smile while I realized I was watching one of Life's Memorable Moments. I wiped away a tear and left the room. I felt like an intruder.

Much, much later, I mentioned how special that was for me and how touched I was. He listened beyond the words and surmised that what I also felt was a little left out, and he decided to remedy that in his own inimitable way. He snuggled up and sniffed around my neck and whispered tenderly, "Is this my Bitch?"

VERY FUNNY, YOU OLD DOG, YOU.

WITNESS FOR THE PERSECUTION

The boy seemed to be around three years old. The man behind him was kicking him in the rear and yelling for him to walk faster, and when he didn't, he'd yank his arm and curse him. There was such hurt in that child's face. I've read the books that tell me that no one can ruin my day unless I give them permission to do so, and I don't think I gave that guy more than a dirty look, but I didn't enjoy the rest of my day at the amusement park.

I said a prayer for the boy that night. I prayed that when he grew up he wouldn't do the same to his kids because he would remember how humiliating it was to be treated unfairly by adults. And then I wondered if I had caught the man at his worst and that was just an isolated incident.

I hope so.

ALMOST GRUDGINGLY, I SAID A PRAYER FOR THE MAN, TOO, BECAUSE I KNEW UNTIL HE GOT RID OF HIS ANGER AND LACK OF SELF-ESTEEM, SO EVIDENT IN HIS DEMEANOR, CHANCES WERE THE LITTLE BOY WOULD CONTINUE TO BE HIS SCAPEGOAT.

THE CHILD ABUSERS

Some of us inflict abuse that is not seen on x-rays. Broken bones and bruises can be easily detected. Psychological abuse surfaces after thirty or forty years sometimes.

Studies have shown that a great majority of parents who abuse their children physically were themselves abused as youngsters and are now repeating the learned behaviors. Is that our excuse for what we often do to our children psychologically? And if it is, at what point are we willing to say, "The pain stops here."

My friends become quite rattled when their kids express their independence by behaving in ways other than those taught at home. Me, too — but then I heave a sigh of relief because I realize that we've done something right to have ended up with such self-sufficient daughters. I secretly rejoice at their courage and innate ability to listen to their gut and do what they feel is right for them. Had they followed our rules and regulations to the letter, I would have known that we had failed.

When they were eight, ten and eleven, they made a giant medal for me with ribbon streamers. It was their way of "making up" after we had exchanged some negative words. The medal read, #1 MOTHER MARTER. In spite of the spelling, I got the message.

> But is it too much to expect them to put
> on a little make-up and not wear jeans
> that look like Goodwill rejects?

YES, MARTYR.

LOVE

I didn't think I'd speak about this subject in the following context. I had planned to develop something concerning male-female relationships.

Then I heard what the middle-aged man said about his twenty-five-year old son, and I got an inkling of what real love is all about. Bernie's eyes glowed with pride and his face broke into a smile as he said, "I'll tell ya. If I could be anyone in this world, I mean ANYONE, I'd be like my son, Randy. Now <u>there</u> is one terrific guy!"

He went on to other subjects but that sentence has been with me for years, and the emotion and caring and admiration in his voice is something indelibly inscribed in my heart.

I suddenly realized that as old as I am, I had not heard a father speak that way about his son. It was such a simple statement — Bernie probably doesn't even remember making it. I wonder if that family knows what a special treasure they are passing on to the next generation? The son is sensitive, creative, loving and caring. Randy is marrying our daughter Rachel, and someone asked me if he was a professional man and if Rachel was marrying into wealth. Randy works at a pizza parlor and Rachel goes to college. I replied that Rachel was marrying one of the wealthiest young men I had ever met who was destined to have great success in life. He comes into our family from parents who cherish him exactly as he is today.

IN A WORLD FULL OF PEOPLE WHO LOVE "IF" OR "WHEN" I CAN'T THINK OF A BETTER DEFINITION FOR "LOVE."

Sexuality

THE GURU

Anyone who's been married fifteen, twenty, twenty-five years and who will not admit that there were times when their marriage got a little tired, will lie to you about other things, too.

It was during a year of my life when I was asking, "Is that all there is?" that I listened intently to a lady who was being interviewed by Merv. She had written a best selling book that gave women hints on being more "total". One of her suggestions was to greet him at the door in a way that would guarantee his not asking, "What's for dinner?" With three kids and a dog that would take some planning.

Finally the day was perfect and I asked him to call me when he was headed home from the office. I told him I had planned something special. At 5:20 he informed me he'd be home in twenty-five minutes.

The frantic scene in the kitchen consisted of a chubby housewife standing stark naked in the middle of her kitchen, wrapping herself in Saran Wrap. (Hey — that's what the expert told me to do! When you're sitting in Miami in your muu-muu dunking Oreos in milk, you know an expert when you see one.)

Unfortunately, the expert didn't know that I needed a lot of instructions. She never told me to wrap each leg *individually*. Many minutes later, I hopped to the front door looking like a 2001 Space Mummy. It was July and the temperature was in the nineties. I wore my quilted robe in order to add to the mystique of the moment.

My husband got caught in traffic and was twenty minutes late. At about the time I thought the morning headlines would read, "HOUSEWIFE DIES OF HEAT STROKE ENCASED IN PLASTIC," the door opened. I put my plan into action. Slowly, deliberately, I let the robe fall to the floor as I looked at him in my most come-hither style, perspiration beading on my face. I caught a glimmer of amused disbelief combined with a tight look around the mouth that said, "If I laugh, I've had it. I must *not* laugh." He stepped back, surveyed the scene with one raised eyebrow, looking very much like Rod Steiger in Doctor Zhivago, spread his arms, and in his most authentic Russian accent bellowed, "You haf had a rough day too, Babushka? Come to me mine leetle sausage."

We laughed so hard it hurt. We were too tickled to even consider a romantic interlude. The combination of heat, extra weight, and tight wrapping had left red welts in bands all around my body that made me look like a zebra with prickly heat. Besides, I couldn't find the end of the Saran Wrap. Can we ever?

That was the day I learned that I run into problems, feel frustrated and don't accomplish much when I act in ways other than what feels natural to me. Candlelight and flowers are my style. The mischevious wench in me wishes I were a little kinky, but I think I'm basically too square for that stuff.

WHEN I BUY WHIPPED CREAM, THE MOST CREATIVE USE I FIND FOR IT IS ON JELL-O. ACCORDING TO SOME BOOKS I'VE READ, THAT MAKES ME AN UNINSPIRED WIMP.

META-COMMUNICATIONS

We have just met. He is witty and charming and good-looking and is asking me to meet him for lunch. No big deal. It's a common occurrence in some women's lives.

I am witty and charming and suddenly feel very beautiful. I certainly didn't feel that way this morning! I am also scared, so I decline the invitation.

He calls me a week later.

By then I have decided what color nightgown I am going to wear when I have a mad, passionate, secret fling with him.

Although I have difficulty breathing when I answer the phone and recognize the voice, I play it very cool. I firmly tell him never to call again. Somehow, without too much being said about it, this stranger and I know we will never be just friends.

I hang up the phone and wonder if I am a coward or a realist.

The flirt in me hopes he will call again.

The wife and mother is thankful he doesn't.

SOMETIMES I FEEL VERY SQUARE IN A VERY ROUND WORLD. IT SCARES ME TO KNOW I AM CAPABLE OF ALMOST ANYTHING. AND IT COMFORTS ME TO KNOW THE CHOICE IS MINE.

BEING THERE

"Not tonight. I've got a headache."

"No problem. Put your head over there in the corner and throw the rest of you over here."

If he knew that 90% of lovemaking is in my head, he wouldn't joke about it. When I just use the body, I'm not really there. We both miss out on a lot. And I transmit that silently to him.

I remember the day I mentally measured the window for new drapes. He suddenly stopped and said, "Hey — if you're alive — will you blink your eyes?"

And yet the part he said was important, the body, was there.

That confirmed my suspicion that passion is much more complex than lust is. Lust screams, "I must." Passion whispers, "How wonderful that you feel the same way, too."

I'VE DECIDED THE CLOSEST THING TO LUST I EVER FEEL CONSISTENTLY, IS MY CRAVING FOR STRAWBERRY CHEESECAKE.

MATURITY

The words were difficult to express, but I thought they needed to be said.   It was our fifteenth wedding anniversary and I had an attack of honesty.

"I love you and adore you but I have something important I need to discuss with you."

He got that look on his face that asked, "NOW what?" I continued.   "I no longer get shaky knees or feel out of breath when you come into a room."

"Lady,"   (there was exasperation in his voice)   "If you want shaky knees and trouble breathing when I come into a room after all these years of marriage and courtship, the only way that's going to happen is if you contract a very severe case of malaria."   His ego was bruised.

Only I knew the rest of the story. I had spent the afternoon with my girlfriend and heard her relate the delights of her affair. I think I was more than a little jealous. I felt I must be missing out on exciting, intriguing moments.

Many years have passed. Her passionate affair is over. My comfortable one continues with my husband. Lately, I feel very rich and not at all deprived.

HAS IT TAKEN YOU AS LONG TO GROW UP?

Family

FLOWER POWER

It is not our enemies who do us the greatest harm. Sometimes we permit our uniqueness and individuality and self-esteem to be eroded little by little, day by day, by those who love us the most. I realized that the day I decided why I did not want flowers at my funeral.

I was to speak at a Conference on Human Rights and as I left the house, I went in to kiss our youngest daughter who was still sleeping, good-bye.

She opened one eye and groaned, "Gross."
I was puzzled. "What's gross?"
"The flowers in your hair, Mom. It's too early for that."
I smiled and headed for the garage. On my way past the kitchen, daughter number two looked up from the morning paper and also communicated with one word, "Tacky."

I stopped smiling. One "gross" and one "tacky" is about all I can take first thing in the morning. As I consulted with the mirror, daughter number three's words haunted me, "How many of the three hundred people there today will have flowers in their hair, Mom? Doesn't that TELL you something?"

I kept the flowers in the hair. I knew it was not too early. If truth be told, it was almost too late.
Many years later, after having done a session on Creative Living for a Board of Realtors, I received a card in the mail. It said, "I want you to know that ever since I heard you speak last week, I've been wearing flowers in my hair."

It was signed, "Wayne Cochran, Realtor."

ARE YOU WEARING THE FLOWERS, OR SMELLING THEM, OR PLANTING THEM, OR SENDING THEM TO OTHERS AND SOMETIMES BUYING THEM FOR YOURSELF OR WILL YOU WAIT UNTIL THE FLORIST DELIVERS THEM-----TO THE FUNERAL HOME?

LITTLE BROTHER

He's a man now.

And sometimes I see too much of Papa in him and that makes me uncomfortable because I have a tendency to act like a little girl around a Papa.

But recently, I found out he wasn't Papa.
This man listened.
And he hugged me when I cried.
And understood silently without too much conversation.
I saw old pain in his eyes — behind the bravado.
There was also a great deal of sensitivity.

I'm glad I finally got to know the real him after all these years. We sat and talked of the unspeakable that we had both kept to ourselves for an entire lifetime. It was very difficult. And very necessary. I'm so thankful we both had the courage to face the dragons and slay them so we could go on joyously with our lives.

Have you taken care of your unfinished business?
It doesn't have to haunt you, unless you give it permission to do so. Of course, you could save yourself the agony of a few hours or days while you undergo a catharsis.

BUT BY DOING THAT, YOU MAY ALSO BE CHOOSING TO CONTINUE TO HURT FOREVER.

83

THE NEW-BORN

It was 1963 and the three-week old baby was turning blue in the bassinet, very obviously choking. The two year old was saying that she was sorry and crying and looking very scared.

I removed a piece of ham from the baby's mouth. Her sister had been eating a sandwich and thought it was a good idea to share a little of what she had.

For some reason, that reminds me of how I feel around people who are so publicly religious and self-righteous. They insist on force-feeding the rest of us their sustenance of meat when our digestive systems can only tolerate milk.

Maybe that's why we choke on it, too. We are still new-born and need more time to develop, that's all. And it has little to do with calendar age.

If they had faith in the Source, they would know that the same illuminations that came to them will come to us when and if we need them enough to reach out.

GOD DOESN'T PLAY FAVORITES.

MY SON, THE DOCTOR

We didn't know it at the time, but when my brother opened his dental office and Mama had an appointment, she would arrive several hours before the allotted time. She sat in the waiting room pretending to read magazines until she could strike up a conversation with the patients waiting their turn.

And always it evolved into glowing recommendations for the wonderful hands this young dentist had and what a charming man he was to do business with. She would even show them the work he had done on her molars.

All that stopped the day my brother, instead of the receptionist, opened the waiting room door. He exclaimed, "Mama! What are you doing here today? Your appointment isn't until tomorrow."

She went in to visit with him and came out a few minutes later. The people in the waiting room applauded her when she left.

Year later, when she told me the story, her eyes were shining.

I'M NOT SURE, BUT I THINK THAT MAY HAVE BEEN ONE OF MAMA'S GREATEST MOMENTS ON EARTH.

THE RICH MAN

He is in his seventies and walks around smiling and shaking hands and saying, "Isn't this a great day?"

And sometimes people stare at him and their faces seem to respond, "What is it with this guy?"

But if they stay around him for a little while, their faces are often transformed and they, too, show a bit of wonder when they realize that the sunset on the beach that evening is indeed extraordinary. And they also delight in the baby gulls on the shore that run away from an unknown invader — an aluminum pie plate shining in the sun.

He's never owned a car or driver's license. He lives in a rented apartment. When he takes his last breath many will smile remembering him. He is the richest man I have ever known.

I, TOO, AM A LITTLE RICHER FOR HAVING EXPER-IENCED SUNSETS THROUGH HIS EYES.

THE GIRL FRIEND

The children were small and we had all returned from a trip to the zoo. The eight kids were running around the house and she suddenly said, "Rosie, when I die, promise me you'll play something Spanish at my funeral." I almost began to joke about her morbidity, but there was something in her eyes that told me this was not the time for humor. I promised.

EIGHT YEARS LATER —

I call her and tell her I'm going to visit her tomorrow. Although I haven't spoken with her in almost a year, I have an urgent, inexplicable and slightly panicky feeling that she could use some company and conversation. She tells me she is not feeling well and wonders if I'll visit her next week instead, when she feels better.

ONE WEEK AFTER THE PHONE CALL —

I visit her and sing the Spanish song — at the funeral home. I wonder if she feels better now? She is dead at forty-two and I look at her five grown children and remember that day at the zoo. Wasn't it yesterday?

I played a rousing Mexican song and I'm sure some people there thought it was the weirdest sight they had ever seen at a funeral. But their opinion didn't matter because I had explained her request to her family and they understood. And I'm sure she was pleased, too. She was one of the people who most encouraged me to sing from the time I was sixteen and I confessed to her that someday I would do something wonderful with music, although I had no idea what that "something" would be.

I know I'm not responsible for anyone else's life, but why didn't I insist on going over the day I called? My heart told me she desperately needed a friend at that precise moment. That will remain one of my life's unanswered questions. I imagine most people have one or two of those.

Once again, I allowed politeness and logic to influence a decision that needed only to be made with the heart.

DO YOU, TOO, FIND YOURSELF REPEATING THE SAME MISTAKES AND RE-LEARNING THE SAME LESSONS?

FRIENDSHIP

How many people would you feel comfortable calling at 3 a.m. if you were lonely and miserable and needed to talk to someone? I can only think of four. That's why although my address book is filled with names, I appreciate how special those four people are.

Don't you wonder about men, and who they turn to in their moments of need? If we're very fortunate, they don't pick up the phone. They reach out and hold on to us to make it through the night. But if we're not there, or if we are the cause of their discomfort, whom do they turn to then?

For too many, the answer is Jack Daniels.

Perhaps that's the greatest harm that's come from raising our sons to believe that big boys don't cry. What happens to the unshed tears, I wonder? Do they fester inside and that toxicity is what contributes to the ulcers, hypertension, arthritis, allergies and angina?

Ah—you say—but....women have been given permission to cry by society and they have the same diseases.

I KNOW.   I DON'T PRETEND TO HAVE THE ANSWERS.   I'M JUST AT A POINT WHERE I AM QUESTIONING WHAT I HAD IGNORED FOR SO LONG.   AND MAYBE THAT'S PROGRESS.

EDUCATION

My greatest teachers were people who did not know they were teaching me anything. The ones who came into the room loaded with books, charts, and audio-visual equipment often left me cold.

I wonder how many of us are "teaching" in some way today because we needed to learn whatever it is we now pass on to others? My programs encourage people to live creatively and make their own kind of music. Would that have been the subject matter if I had not needed to learn about that for myself?

The hearing-impaired girl who picked up the vibrations of the guitar although she couldn't hear the music — the man in the burn ward, so disfigured I could only look into his mournful eyes in order to communicate — the man who was paralyzed from the neck down and couldn't swat the fly off his nose — and the little old lady who sang a song in the ward at the nursing home (the first time she had uttered a word in the year and a half she had been there) — they were my greatest teachers.

And so was the man who sat across the desk and let me know quietly and with a wonderful sparkle in his eyes that he thought I was a person of worth. When I saw him years later, the sparkle was gone and he looked sadder. Was it nothing more than projection or did he forget to sing his own songs while he was so busy coaching others to sing theirs?

I've forgotten many things and many people in my life, but the teachers who transmitted something to me on a level that transcended paper and pen are with me forever. Are you a schoolteacher? You will never know how much of an influence you have been to that girl you put your arm around. She never forgot you told her she was pretty.

UNTIL THEN, ALL SHE USUALLY HEARD PRIOR TO YOUR KIND WORDS WAS HOW FAT SHE WAS.

"HEY, MAN, LIKE WOW!"

"Bubble-in the card," he said, as I registered for college in my mid-thirties. It was as if he were speaking a foreign language in the Land of Computers. After getting through the maze of registration, I felt I could do anything though I wondered if the material would be over my head.

My fears were unfounded. What was difficult to comprehend was the language. While we sit in suburbia, there is a whole other world out there, and they speak differently than we do.

"THAT'S BAAAAAD!" he said. What he meant was, "Terrific!"

"I CRASHED IN HIS PAD" translated into, "I slept in his apartment."

"I'M GONNA CHECK OUT MY LIDS" meant, "I'm going to take a nap."

I'm a very quick-study. Before long I was saying, "That's cool." My daughters cringed and disowned me that day.

BUT I COULD DIG IT 'CAUSE I KNEW WHERE THEY WERE COMIN' FROM.

THE SYSTEM

She was one of those professors who hang loose. Jeans and sandals were her style, and she was a delight to watch in action. She still had fire and sparkle in her eyes, and although she worked within the system she seemed to be on the outside looking in. She inspired us with the possibilities open to those who did not follow rules that were personally meaningless.

Then the final paper was due, and I watched her turn into an automaton before my eyes. She instructed us as to the size of the margins, the length of the paper and the proper form for listing our sources — just like the other teachers. I had expected so much more. After all, she had spent a semester reminding us what nonsense most of that was and the importance of capturing the essence instead of being guided by the form of things.

I began my paper by stating that if I followed her instructions about the requirements for the paper, I would be proving that I had not learned a thing in her class.
She gave me an "A".
We both knew I had learned her lessons well.

That reminds me of something I feel strongly about: the most under-rated, under-paid profession is that of a teacher, when you consider the impact some of them make on our lives. A good, enthusiastic, caring one may very well be the architect of temples that time does not erode. Think back on your school days and chances are you can remember teachers who made all the difference in your life. Did you ever tell her or him?

IS IT TOO LATE TO LOOK THEM UP TODAY?

93

strangers

WISDOM

Some look for philosophers between covers of books at the library.

I find them on bus benches.

There is something about the old man with the beret that fascinates me, so I stop and we talk for a long time. He boards his bus, I continue on my way and we shall never see each other again. And yet, he is with me, still.

I stare at the numbers on his arm and he tells me he was one of many in Buchenwald. He says, "Life itself is beautiful. It is what is inside of you and nothing and no one can kill that — only you. I live for today, not in the past. There is no future in living in the past."

Ordinarily, I would say that I am not absolutely, positively sure of anything. But today I have met him and today I am absolutely, positively sure that we must never again permit a situation to exist that fosters the categorizing and numbering of human beings.

ESPECIALLY WHEN WE DO IT IN OUR MINDS.

ANONYMOUS ANGELS

There are people whom you and I depended on at certain moments in our lives that we have never forgotten, and in some cases — we never even knew their names.

When I was ten and the doctor who stitched my arm was congratulated for doing such a great job, I knew who the healer had been: the nurse who assured me I was not going to die. She kissed and hugged me when I was hysterical with fright. I'll bet that wasn't in the curriculum when she was in school. I've never forgotten her.

And I don't even know who she was.

I GUESS IN SOME RELATIONSHIPS IDEN-TIFICATION IS SUPERFLUOUS.

INTELLIGENCE

He has been waiting to shake my hand in the back of the crowd that surrounds me and finally approaches with some hesitancy. He squints at me through his thick glasses, gazes at the guitar with admiration and fascination, and the little old man asks, curiously, "Tell me, dollink. Does it matter vere you put de fingars?"

I smile. "Not too much. Mostly, it matters where you put the heart."

He straightens up immediately because he has understood and reaches out and hugs me tight.

Years later I tell the story to an acquaintance. She contorts her face in disbelief. "How stupid! He just thought you could put the hand anywhere on the guitar and get music? I can't believe it!"

She missed the point completely.

I forgot her a long time ago.

I SHALL ALWAYS REMEMBER HIM.

PREJUDICE

"Hell," he says, "we ain't prejudiced! Why we got two o' them Jew boys in our Christian school!" I listen to him and know we will never be very good friends. I feel an antipathy towards the man that does not have words. It just hangs there like a bad smell.

It surprises me to find prejudice within myself.

And what makes it more ridiculous to me is that my prejudice is against people who are prejudiced.

SOMETIMES I'M A GREAT DISAPPOINTMENT TO MYSELF.

GAY AND GRAY

.

It was my job as the professor's research associate to conduct interviews with the population he was studying. We worked for almost two years investigating the adaptation to aging by the older male homosexual. The results were so fascinating, the case histories I wrote were included in a book with the above title.

Years later I figured out how much I had actually earned for that work, based on the hundreds of hours devoted to it, and it came out to about fifty cents per hour. It was also the most valuable, meaningful work I did as a social worker.

What did a Spanish lady with three kids and a husband learn during those years of taping interviews in gay bars, and homes of gays, and at the university office? That people are people. What worries them about growing older are the same things that concern you and me.
I haven't forgotten one person from that period in my life. They touched me forever, and my life has been enriched by their trust in me and the sharing they did so that fear could be dispelled through understanding.

I'm not sure the world is ready to hear this. Many of you reading this page are being turned off. Since the subject incenses so many, it might be more prudent not to mention it at all and pretend it doesn't exist. But if I did that, those two years would have been wasted.

Some of the best and warmest hugs I have ever gotten in my life came from these old, gay men. Me. A woman. Are you surprised?

I WASN'T. MAYBE THAT'S WHY THEY FELT COMFORTABLE GIVING THEM TO ME. HUGS DON'T HAVE A SEXUAL PREFERENCE OR MAKE A SOCIAL STATEMENT.

The Past

THE SILENT SCREAM

We gripe about the petty things of today because it is safe to do so. It is the traumas of yesterday that we have forgotten that disturb us the most. The song that tells us what is too painful to remember also says that we sometimes choose to forget.

Unfortunately, though "forgotten," it is still there. It is only when the information surfaces that we can then deal with it. The timing has to be just right. You won't know when that is, but your psyche will. And after it is all remembered, sometimes the most we can do with those persistent shadows is forget them again.

Hopefully, by that time maturity, forgiveness and under-standing may have been added, so the pain can be tolerated, accepted and finally alleviated.

DIG DEEP FOR YOUR MEMORIES, BUT REMEMBER, THE ONES THAT REALLY MATTER CANNOT BE FOUND IN THE OLD TRUNK IN THE ATTIC OR THE SHOE BOX WITH THE YELLOWED PHOTOGRAPHS.

GRASS

When I was young, grass was something Easter eggs could hide in.   And children rolled on.   And fathers mowed.   I would walk home from school and take three blades and make dozens of tiny green braids that I pinned to my hair.   I like to think Bo Derek's future hairdresser saw me one day and the rest is history.

Today, grass is something *people* hide in.

I WONDER IF THE WORD WILL EVER AGAIN CONJURE UP MEMORIES OF PICNICS AND EASTER EGG HUNTS OR IF THAT HAS NOW CHANGED FOREVER?

GHOSTS AND GOBLINS

It was Halloween, and I was a teenager just moved from New York to Miami. The doorbell rang, and a little pirate shouted, "Trick or Treat!"

He was holding a shopping bag out in front of him and grinned at me as I stared back, a little perplexed. I hesitated, but finally I reached into the bag and took a piece of candy. I smiled and thanked him profusely. "What a wonderful thing to do! Thank you so much!"

He backed away, staring blankly at me as he retreated. Although I was fifteen years old, I had never heard of that game.

When I closed the door and explained to my little brother that I had asked for an extra candy for him, too, he was flabbergasted. "You Dummy! He wanted you to put candy IN his bag — not take some OUT!"

I didn't know. What rock had I been hiding under all those years? If only the little pirate had explained it to me.

Sometimes I feel that in our own adult way, we're playing a similar game today. I come to you for candy and you end up taking mine instead — if I allow it.

I guess one of the most valuable lessons I've learned came from that lady who very patiently taught me it was O.K. to say "no" and not lose love because of my decision.

AND ANY LOVE THAT I LOST, I DIDN'T REALLY HAVE. AND THE OTHERS WEREN'T WORTH KEEPING. THE PRICE WAS TOO HIGH.

YESTERDAY'S TAPE AND TODAY'S HYPE

There are those who pay six hundred dollars for a brief-case and enjoy it. And they feel they deserve the best. I have too much old guilt for that.

There isn't a time I go into a store that carries items made by Cartier and Hermes that I don't marvel at people who can walk in and pay those prices and actually enjoy their purchase. It must be something in the genes, not just the money in the jeans. Although sometimes my wallet can take it, my head can't or won't.

As I was growing up, I observed people who would wash the used aluminum foil to use it again. And saved the little brown lunch bag for tomorrow, neatly folded for recycling. I didn't realize it at the time, but they were leaving indelible impressions.

Just once, I'd like to go into a shop, buy something outrageously expensive, and not look at the price tag.

THE TRICK WILL BE TO REALLY ENJOY IT AFTERWARD.

GIFTS

We miss the boat when we shop for gifts for our children in toy stores.

I remember an old, thin lady who made lemon meringue pies that stood four inches high. And while she baked, she would give me pieces of dough, and I would make snowmen and animals.

There wasn't a toy I was ever given that I recall with as much love and affection and meaning as those pieces of dough.

But we only realize that forty years later.

HER LEGACY? THERE ISN'T A TIME I LOOK AT A LEMON MERINGUE PIE THAT I DON'T THINK OF HER AND SMILE.

THE HOME TOWN NEIGHBOR

I pop in unexpectedly, and she is so happy to see me after all these years. She invites me to return that night, and she will make my favorite dish for dinner. She still remembers. I go back and enjoy that meal more than any I've ever had. We sit in the kitchen, and it feels like home again. I intend to write and tell her all that, and I begin the letter several times, but I never mail it.

That surprises me. It is usually so easy for me to drop someone a line. I think I'm embarrassed at the intensity of love I feel for someone I haven't associated with for over thirty-five years. I'm not sure she'll understand.

I wonder why that family meant so much to me?
Did you have someone in your life like that, too?
Maybe our emotions don't need reasons, especially when they are stored in the heart of a lonely child.

I hope she reads this someday because for reasons known only to the little girl I was, it overwhelms me to express my appreciation out loud for those cherished times.

WORDS OFTEN FAIL ME WHEN THE UNDERLYING EMOTIONS ARE STRONGEST.

"A LITTLE CHILD SHALL LEAD THEM"

Whenever I read that line, I would visualize a youngster taking me by the hand and saying something to me that would open my eyes to a great truth.

Sometimes it was a blond little girl or a freckled boy and they were always cute. Then one night I had a dream that made it very clear to me that the child that leads us is within each one of us. It is the little kid we used to be that is always there in spirit. It's the one who knows the answers instinctively and is not misled by words or pomp and circumstance and cuts through all the facades. (The sophisticated adult we become resists paying attention to that child. After all, what does he or she know? Not much about Pucci or Gucci, granted.) What haunted me for a long time was that the little girl in my dream was not cute or freckled. She looked terribly frightened and her eyes had that dark sunken look we see in pictures of concentration camp victims. I imagine there are those who would say, "Come on — it couldn't have been that bad."

Today, the woman I've become doesn't think so either, but that little girl sure did and that was all that mattered then. It's great to see her so happy and smiling today. She was a good little kid and deserves the fun times that had been postponed for so long.

That is why, whenever I see a bumper sticker that asks, HAVE YOU HUGGED YOUR KID TODAY? it has a special meaning for me because I know, beyond a doubt, that at long last, I definitely have.

How about you? Have you made friends with all aspects of yourself? I don't mean just the lovable, competent you. I'm talking about the petty, scared, inadequate and pessimistic you, also. And especially, have you become a good friend of the very young person you were long, long ago?

BECAUSE UNTIL YOU DO THAT, IT MAY BE VERY DIFFICULT FOR YOU TO BECOME A GOOD FRIEND TO ANYONE ELSE.

ROOTS

We visited the old home town and the plush car seemed strangely out of place in that narrow street. It was a happy day and I was showing our family where I had grown up.

"See girls — how close together the houses were? I could unlatch the window screens and hand toys to my friend next door." I was unprepared for the emotions that surfaced in me with that remark. Suddenly I felt like a sad little girl again.

I remembered Mary. She was ten and I was eight. Often, very late at night, we heard her scream an unpunctuated litany: "Please Daddy. No Daddy. No more Daddy, please!" And with each whack and snap of the belt (wielded in silent rage because Mary's voice was the only one heard), I cried. And Mama did, too. As we clung to each other she would whisper, "Don't listen. Cover your ears. Get away from the window. It's none of our business. It's not nice . . . . ."

And when it got very bad, usually on Friday nights when he came home drunker than usual, I would stifle my sobs with a pillow and muzzle my agony with a sheet. A few days later while playing with Mary, I saw the bruises. But she never said anything about them and I was taught to be a polite little girl so I never mentioned them either. Thirty-eight years later Mary is in a mental institution.

Forgive us, Mary. We knew not what we did by doing nothing. We were ignorant but not insensitive. Maybe we were scared, too. It wasn't until I was grown that I knew crying for you was not enough.

Child abuse was not a term known on our block in 1944. The freshly starched lace curtains served as iron walls that allowed very little to disrupt our safe worlds within.

Today, we live half an hour from the old neighborhood. I go out of my way not to pass by that street. There is too much of Mary still there for me. And maybe too much Little Rosita, too. What did I learn from knowing you, Mary?

I LEARNED NOT TO ALLOW MY POLITENESS TO GET IN THE WAY OF MY HEARTFELT OUTRAGE. I MAKE WAVES.

DICHOTOMIES

Does it bother you to know that what you do so well professionally, you sometimes don't do well at all personally? It does me.

I traveled to the city where he lived with the intent of saying goodbye. Although he had been ill for many years, I felt an uneasiness about waiting a month, when it would have been more convenient for me to visit him. I followed the inner voice that doesn't give me explanations, but has seldom steered me wrong.

I sat by his bed and made small talk, waiting for my opportunity to put all my communication skills to work. He was watching a John Wayne western and commented, "He's got cancer, you know. When he goes, I go. I'm not going to live past this year." I was beyond the point of playing the game of denial. I nodded my head. I reached for his hand. I wanted to say so much that had been unexpressed for so long. He tightened up and pulled back. Whatever it was I was thinking, he didn't want to hear. That angered me. We were repeating the same behaviors, even to the end. Then, it occurred to me that he had as much right NOT to listen, as I had to speak. Maybe he couldn't handle his feelings as well as I. Maybe that was one of the influences in my life that impelled me not to be afraid of expressing my feelings.

I sat there and said everything I so desperately needed to say, but I said it all to myself, silently. You see, the important thing was that I express it, not that he actually hear it. He suddenly became very animated and exclaimed, "Watch this scene! Here's where he gets the bad guys!" His eyes remained glued to the TV and although I tried to catch his glance again, I never did.

For years, people have told me I communicate with my eyes. That day I learned that I need to have another pair of eyes in order for that to be true. I'm only fifty percent responsible for what transpires.

Then I did something for which I had no training. I gave up. I leaned back, relaxed, watched the movie, and casually said goodbye. I watched him for a long time from the door because somehow I knew I would not see him alive again. I left without him ever having heard what I had come three hundred miles to verbalize. Somehow, though, it seemed all right. At least, I <u>had</u> said it.

Three weeks later, one day after John Wayne died, Papa died, too.

SO LONG, PILGRIM. IF I HAD BEEN YOUR SCRIPT WRITER I WOULD HAVE WRITTEN A NEATER, HAPPIER ENDING AND A STORY WITH ONLY GOOD GUYS.

The
Unexpected

ON DOING AND BEING

Frank Sinatra croons, "Do-Be-Do-Be-Do" and as I listen with an ear accustomed to hearing the usual in an unusual way, I hear a Universal Truth.

How often do we DO in order to BE?

We attend universities to obtain a degree that will allow us to be what we want to be. But first we have to DO all kinds of things we innately know are meaningless, but look good on paper, in order to get the right letters after our name. And while we are so busy doing, we grow old and forget to have fun along the way.

Ever since I decided to just BE and let my doing be a reflection of who and what I already was — my life has changed. What will it take to get you to go from "three to get ready" to "four to go"? More money? A hair transplant? Twenty pounds off the scale? Ten years off your age with the help of cosmetic surgery? Divorce? Marriage?

For me, it was something more urgent: a diagnosis from a doctor that I was not ready to hear.

IF I HAD NOT BEEN SCARED INTO IT, I MIGHT HAVE DIED WITH THE MUSIC IN ME.

THE YIN AND YANG OF IT

Just lately, I've realized that illness can be an opportunity. It impels us to take stock. It helps us to know what is to be cherished and what needs to be discarded. It is also an educator. For instance, I've learned that whatever goes wrong with my body, I have been instrumental in bringing about. It does not operate independently of my emotions. I needed to let go of a great deal of inner rage at what I felt were injustices that life had heaped upon me or others I loved. I had to recognize who it was I resented, and forgive them. And I needed to forgive myself, too. Knowing that, I have some control over how long I remain ill. This is not an easy admission for me to make. I do so here in the hope that there is something in my experience you will identify with, if you find yourself in a similar place. If all this sounds a little nebulous, it is. I have no need or desire to go into details of symptoms and diagnosis. That is important only to me and my immediate family.

Something very meaningful has happened, though. And I don't think I would have gotten in touch with it unless I had experienced the fright and hopelessness I once did, when nothing seemed to alleviate the condition. I now know I can take charge of my life. The illness can run me or I can work and live and love and laugh around it. And something tells me if I do that long enough and don't sabotage myself with destructive thoughts and habits that will exacerbate the condition, I may emerge from all this with a great deal more than I had when it began.

How interesting that the illness manifested itself when I decided to quit my safe job, start my own business, and travel. I decided it was separation anxiety. I had a conversation with the disease. I told it that if it was rearing its ugly head in order to keep me from doing something I was unsure about and a little scared of attempting, (though not too much, because my inner clock and the spirit said, GO!) it wasn't going to work. I would not use poor health as an excuse for not getting my music out. I decided that when it had served its purpose, it would probably depart. Six years later, I'm delighted to find that is exactly what is happening.

Some of you are thinking, "This gal has learned how to make lemonade out of lemons." Not true. I can't stand lemonade. I simply learned how to plant another tree of something I truly want and like. I threw the lemons away. No use passing on to others what I didn't consider good enough for me.

If you have a health problem, don't despair. First let go of the anger. Then, let go of the illness, gently. Maybe it is your body's way of getting you to pay attention so that you, too, will make some changes.

IS IT EASY? YOU KNOW THAT ANSWER AS WELL AS I. BUT REMEMBER, THE QUALITY AND MAYBE EVEN THE QUANTITY OF YOUR LIFE MAY DEPEND ON YOUR DECISION.

CLOSE ENCOUNTERS

It happened at a time when I was hurting so much psychologically, I questioned whether I wanted to wake up tomorrow. I attempted to drive across six lanes of traffic at an intersection without a light. Nevertheless, they called it an accident. Damage to my car exceeded several thousand dollars and I was unconscious for twenty minutes. The doctor on the scene told me afterward that he could not get a pulse and that my pupils were fixed and dilated. Witnesses said my tongue was hanging to the side. When I awoke, I felt I had just blinked my eyes and the only reason I returned from where I had been was that I heard our daughter scream my name with anguish unlike anything I had ever heard before. Her voice seemed to pull me back and I knew then I had not finished my work here yet, so I returned, almost casually, and wondering what all the fuss was about. That was nine years ago.

To this day I recall the sensation of being catapulted through a dark and swirling tunnel and the indescribable brightness of the light in the place where I finally arrived. What was different about this light was that I was not able to detect where it began or ended. It permeated everything and seemed to be the embodiment of knowledge because there wasn't one thing I asked that was not immediately answered to my satisfaction. It is taking me longer to describe the event than it took to actually happen because time, as we know it, does not exist there. I remember especially that communication was accomplished without forming words with our lips or using our ears to hear. Thoughts were transmitted back and forth at breakneck speed and although I knew there was a presence there, it did not seem necessary for this entity to have a body like the one we use on earth. The light was enough. Our senses were so refined, we saw and heard without need of the usual apparatus, including bodies. You and I both know this sounds like something for the next issue of the *NATIONAL ENQUIRER* so that is why I confided only in a few friends and some family. Many of them looked at me very strangely. It sounded as crazy to me as it obviously did to them, but that does not change the fact that it DID happen. I will not deny that I heard my mother's voice exclaim, "Live! I'm fine! There are no accidents! I was ready to leave! Enjoy!" Many years later I read books that spoke of "out-of-body-experiences" and people who claimed to observe themselves dying. I never felt I died. I just knew, without a doubt, that I had visited another dimension and by doing that, this life and this earth suddenly became more precious. The world looks different to me now and the people in it are much more dear. What did I learn about dying on that sojourn? Nothing. I DID learn a great deal about living. If I were asked to sum up the experience in three words, they would be: I understand now.

My emotional dictionary has been revised and up-dated so that words like "security" no longer mean the same to me. And now, when grief comes into my life, it visits briefly without taking up permanent residency as it did before this experience.

The incident encouraged me to become a risk-taker and much more of a hugger than I was before. Just the fact that you and I are on this earth at the same time is reason enough for me to care about you. I work on projects because they are fascinating to me and I know I can contribute something, without being concerned about "making a living." Life has become an adventure. The eventual financial remuneration for my work has come about almost incidentally. I look into people's eyes and know whether or not to form business liaisons with them. I run in the other direction when, despite all the right facades, the vibrations tell me not to bother. Along the way I have found that the more people I help accomplish their goals and turn their dreams into realities, the easier it becomes for me to attain mine. I am no longer competing. Instead, I am sharing the abundance there is for all because now I know it is limitless.

It has taken me many years to assimilate what happened to me the day of that accident. Although I knew immediately that something very important had taken place, I could not figure it out. All I could do was attempt to explain it to others. And then one day I stopped doing that. I don't ever mention this from the platform. It seems too private. I think I'm doing so here because the printed page provides me with a measure of safety. You see, although that day helped me transform my life and nothing seems the same, and the news seems too good to keep to myself, the skeptic in me lives on. I know and believe it myself but fully understand why you would not.

THERE IS DANGER, THOUGH, IN SMILING AT ELDERLY MEN IN HOTEL LOBBIES AS IF I LOVED THEM. ONE STRANGER SAID TO ME, "I THINK YOU'D BETTER TAKE YOUR HAND OFF MY KNEE. I'M NOT THAT OLD!"

AFTERTHOUGHT

Obviously, I've forgotten or am choosing to ignore a lot of what I learned that day. The proof is that I'm writing this book when I now know how unimportant these projects we give so much time and energy to are — ultimately.

Be patient with me. Some lessons are taking me a lifetime to put into practice and accept. I promise to have as much consideration for your inconsistencies.

The most important message I gleaned is that there are doors only we can open for ourselves. No amount of explanation by someone else will convince us or suffice. But I'm only human. I don't always do and live what I know to be true — so here goes:

> When you and I become less scared of dying,
> we become more brave about really living.
> How do we know a private miracle has taken
> place? When that which was impossible yesterday
> is done effortlessly today, with little thought
> given to tomorrow. Each day is embraced and
> appreciated. Today IS life.

Many of you reading this have experienced mini-deaths. A divorce. The loss of a loved one. A betrayal. Profound disappointments. Business reversals. Lost fortunes. Unrealized dreams. Harsh realities. Painful illnesses.

Through it all, I hope you've known that the darkness is not to be feared. It is nothing more than a door. Although our tendency is to run away from it, what we most need to do is lean into it and allow ourselves to be transported to the Light. It is unfortunate, but the darkness seems to be the only road available in order to get to a better place.

MY WISH FOR YOU? THAT YOU, TOO, WILL DIE A LITTLE SO YOU WILL KNOW HOW TO LIVE A LOT.

THE MUSIC LESSON

I knew the guitar practice was paying off when I detected callouses on my fingers and the chord placement was almost automatic, without too much concentrated effort needed before I made a decision. I've practiced being a loving, caring, human being for a long time and I can only hope I haven't developed callouses on my soul. Some of the sessions have been very difficult. No one knows better than I that I've hit more than a few sour notes — usually when I allowed my pride, or anger, or ego to get in the way. What I will concentrate on today, though, are the times I sang in perfect pitch. I know there are many beautiful songs still left to sing and share.

If the ones on these pages made sense to you and if you heard a bit of yourself in some of these tunes, reach out and take my hand. There is no reason for us to continue to sing alone.

My dear friend, forget the fact that you won't hit the high notes. Leave those to Pavarotti. Sing your song up to the point you're able to, comfortably. Resist waiting until you overcome all your fears and have all your answers. That time may not come while you are on this earth.

Trust yourself. From the time I was a child, my dreams terrified me. Over a period of many years I became aware of incidents that happened, many years later, in exactly the way they had appeared in my dreams. The anxiety that produced is difficult to describe. After my "close encounter of the personal kind" I learned to accept what the dreams were saying. I learned to trust them, embrace them, make allies of them instead of enemies, and by so doing, their need to exist has diminished. Because I pay much more attention to myself now, while awake, I imagine the sleep communications are no longer as necessary. Lately, they have informed me of some absolutely wonderful and fantastic moments that are ahead in my life. I've already "enjoyed the happening before it has happened!" And the sadness ahead that I see also? I accept it. It comes with the territory of being human, vulnerable and alive.

Don't hold back. Get on with it.

IN THE CHORUS OF LIFE, THE MUSIC IS YOU!

NEW

A THREE HOUR, THREE TAPE CASSETTE PROGRAM
A TALKING AND SINGING BOOK!

IF . . . . You have spent years striving for perfection and are now willing to settle for excellence

IF . . . . You are a dreamer who knows possibility thinking precedes dynamic realities

IF . . . . You know you have often lived a lot, only after you have died a little

IF . . . . You've lived through the sad and are ready to embrace and enjoy the glad

THIS CASSETTE PROGRAM AND BOOK ARE FOR YOU!

"She talks as if she has been peeking over my shoulder as I've lived my life."

Rosita speaks, one-on-one, elaborating many of the messages shared in her guide to thinking less and feeling more, THE MUSIC IS YOU. She reveals much she does not share from the platform. Some of the concepts, set to music and performed for enthusiastic audiences, will tickle your funny-bone, whisper to your soul, and cause your heart to rejoice.

"Your wisdom and unique perception of life have added to mine. I am more for it."
LEO F. BUSCAGLIA, Ph. D.

"Rosita's cassette program is one of the finest personal growth programs on the market. I recommend it without reservation."
MIKE FRANK, C.S.P.
Past President, National Speakers Association
President, Speakers Unlimited

"Rosita must be a special angel, on leave from heaven. Her words and thoughts have that magical ability to turn anyone's darkest day into glowing hours filled with new hope, new confidence, and new faith. What a miracle!"
OG MANDINO, Author and Lecturer

LIVE!
FOR THE
WINNER IN YOU!

ROSITA PEREZ

TOPICS: Life Changing Events • The Search for Self • Image vs The Real Thing • Success Theory • Overcoming Addictions • Education • Marriage • Sexuality • First Impressions • Children • Personal Ordeals • Accepting Sorrow • Celebrating Life • The Child Within •Beyond Fear

READ THE BOOK - LISTEN TO THE CASSETTES

A **SOUND** INVESTMENT

A POWERFUL MUSICAL JOURNEY INTO SELF-FULFILLMENT THAT WILL HELP YOU **TUNE IN** TO YOUR UNTAPPED POTENTIAL

MAIL ORDER TO:
TRUDY KNOX, PUBLISHER
168 WILDWOOD DRIVE
GRANVILLE, OHIO 43023   TOTAL

Please send _____ Cassette Albums @**$29.95** $ _____

Please send _____ copies of the book, "The Music Is You"
@**$10.00** $ _____

Add for postage, $1.00 for one or two books, $2.50 for each album.
Please add additional postage for delivery outside United States.
Ohio residents, add 5½% sales tax. $ _____

ENCLOSED IS CHECK OR MONEY ORDER, U.S. Funds only.
Payable to Trudy Knox, Publisher   **TOTAL** $ _____
SEND TO:

NAME_____

                                                APT #,
ADDRESS _____ SUITE # _____

CITY _____ STATE_____

PHONE ( )_____ ZIP _____
PLEASE ALLOW 4-6 WEEKS DELIVERY